34

THE

TO

A commuter's tales of

adventure and misadventure

Julian Kirkman-Page

A mallard ate my mother!

From Ghosts to the Galapagos; from Rocks to Rockets;
and from Space to 'Spaced out'.

14 true tales of comic mayhem, mistaken identity, haunted houses, the supernatural, and a great deal of mischief before CCTV came along and spoilt everything.

Our author is a train commuter trying to make good use of the otherwise dead time to study for a distance learning science degree. Instead, the trials and tribulations of the daily grind between home and London Bridge station force him to reflect upon an unusual life filled with adventure and misadventure.

EPIGRAPHS

Through the carriage window,

I watch the world drift calmly by;

As I ride the parallel lines,

Towards a pre-set destination;

But deep in my mind,

I glide past galaxies,

In a parallel universe,

With no beginning, no rules, and no termination.

Com-mute   (verb)

To change a penalty for a less severe one

e.g. to commute a death penalty to a life in prison

DEDICATION

To my darling wife, Lolly

List of Train Journeys

MAP ONE

Relevant 'outer' stations on the South-East
England rail network

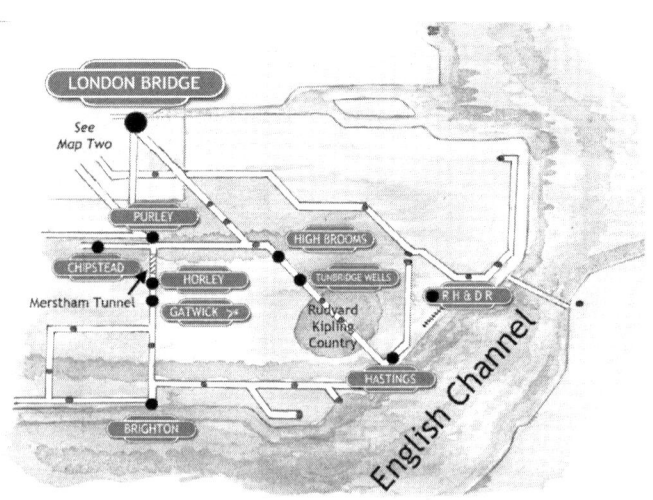

Relevant 'inner' stations on the South-East England rail network

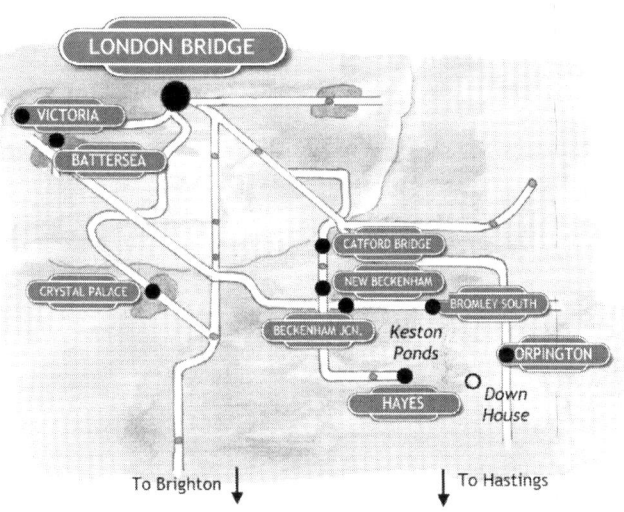

I am fifty years of age, a businessman, and a rail commuter bound for London Bridge station. But this fine early morning, Dear Reader; I am in the guise of a student. After countless years of sitting, staring aimlessly out of the train window, I am now attempting to employ the time usefully by studying for a degree with the Open University. This is quite a lofty ambition for someone who was 'asked to leave' school and who ended up with few genuine qualifications. The driving force behind this volte-face was watching my eldest daughter march proudly across the university stage, to shake hands with the Dean at her own graduation, and my throwing down the gauntlet with a casual 'I can do that' comment. I am also remembering how hard I found it to concentrate and retain any knowledge, especially in an environment with so many distractions and daily annoyances, and especially as I am already frustrated by the train having arrived late at my station, as per usual.

The subject I have chosen to read is Geosciences, which literally embraces everything from the tiniest quantum particle; to atoms and molecules; to rocks and mountains; to the make-up and history of planet Earth; to stars and galaxies; and even ponders what if anything lies beyond our vast expanding Universe.

Sitting opposite me is a youngish gentleman studying *his* stars in the newspaper. I say 'gentleman' out of innate politeness, and for all you know he may well be just such a rare breed. However, the quality of the journal he is reading (for which a vocabulary amounting to at least fifty words is required to gain any sort of qualitative understanding), the tattooed words on his hands which possibly help as a reminder of at least two, the pierced ears, the dirty smelly clothes, the nicotine stains on his fingers, his filthy feet being on the seat, and the ring in his lip detract somewhat from the likelihood; but I am never one to judge people or things at face value.

Now I know most females love to read their stars (unless they are astronomers), but it's rare you see a male read them in public, although I think most men (and I am no exception) are probably closet astrologers and will peek at them in private given half a chance.

The Unlikely Gentleman is smiling to himself so he either has wind, or it's obviously good news for him. He is going to have the exact same ambiguously pleasant things dictate his day as a half a billion other people on the planet, but the exact same ambiguously pleasant things give him a nice sense of wellbeing. It's probably also good news that Madame Astra has noticed that Pluto (although no longer a planet having been demoted to 'dwarf planet' in 2006), is currently in his constellation and thereby having a considerable influence on the day's good fortune.

I was born on the last day of April 1957 at Bromley Hospital in South London, sometime early that morning. Had I been able to read my horoscope I would have found that the 30th of April was an auspicious day for me, but not so favourable for Herr Adolf Hitler who, my parents made a regular point of telling me, killed himself exactly twelve years earlier (like most stubborn children in my youth, who insisted on getting their own way, 'Little Hitler' seemed to be a favourite pet name; I just happened to have more of a claim to the title). I have no idea what planet was in the constellation Taurus at the time of my birth, but I do know now that the morning mail train passing nearby the hospital at that exact moment, would have had far more gravitational influence on my life than even something as massive as the planets: Mercury; Venus; Mars; Jupiter; Saturn; Uranus; Neptune; and little Pluto combined!

If that sounds somewhat technical, it is because the book open before me and that I am supposed to be studying, is entitled *Sun and Stars*. I have already learnt many theories about things I can't possibly influence; for instance, that the photon radiation illuminating my book only left the surface of the Sun some 8.3 minutes ago, but that it probably took some two hundred thousand years for it to reach the Sun's surface from its core. Coincidentally, I have been on this train for about 8.3 minutes, and it too seemed to take thousands of years to turn up. I can't do much to influence that either.

13

The real challenge for me with this degree, is not remembering such useful everyday facts, but staying focused and not wandering off on some irrelevant reverie; especially as the Unlikely Gentleman has now deliberately part-covered my book with his grimy paper, and is giving me a threatening look. I have also noticed that his eyes are so very close together that they remind me of a time many, many years ago…

As a very young boy I could be likened to a ball. I was obviously therefore very round, with chubby arms and legs, blonde hair on my very round head (the hair would eventually go black, the head would remain very round and never suit a hat), and large dimples in my cheeks which all Mother's buxom lady friends liked to pinch and then laugh sweetly to each other when I started crying. For some reason I was always dressed in either a red or a blue sailor suit complete with a hat, and was consequently given such affectionate names as 'Baby Dumpling', 'Boo Boo', or 'Master Spy' after the fat alien featuring in the then TV series Fireball XL5 (you can Google this character, it is not a pleasant sight.) The key thing however, and what made all Mother's buxom pinching lady friends jealous, was that I was a good child - an extremely good child. I would carry with me wherever I was taken, a tiny suitcase within which was a tiny train-set from the American firm, Lone Star. Whilst the ladies nattered away and pretended to like each other, I would lay the tiny metal track, put together the tiny metal station and push round the tiny metal engines and carriages for hours, making childish train noises and generally looking as adorable as possible. I know I was a complete joy to Mother because my elder brother Paul had been and was a complete nightmare.

By the time I was born, Dad was doing well as a Chartered Accountant, we lived in a nice semi-detached suburban house with a small but well stocked garden, and life was as picture-book fifties as can be imagined. Five years previously however, when Paul was born, Dad was still getting over the trauma of six years fighting the Japanese in Burma and coming back weighing seven stone (he didn't like the food); Britain was in post-war rationing mode, and they were living in a small flat above Dad's uncle's house in South London. These kind relations not only charged an extortionate rent, they allowed only a handful of coal per day (hence Mother froze in the Winter, only lighting the fire when Dad was due home), and they hated children, so Paul had to be kept quiet and well behaved. Quiet and well-behaved however were never imprinted on Paul's DNA and from birth he had been programmed not to sleep, not to keep still, not to not be loud and to generally get up to as much mischief and mayhem as was possible. As a consequence Mother spent most days pushing Paul around London tied into a push-chair (he wouldn't be put in reins), apologising with tears in her eyes to people for his behaviour (she always felt she was to blame) and then helping strap and rope him into bed once Father got home. I was never strapped and roped into bed but they did tuck the sheets in tight so I couldn't move, but this never bothered me, and in fact it was decades until I could adapt to the looseness of a duvet.

I was devoted to my elder brother, forever wishing he would hurry home from school, and then following him wherever he went and putting up with the fact he always had to be in charge, was always bored and therefore up to no good, and that he was as my mother's friends called him, 'a dog in the manger', preferring to exterminate his toys (including a beautiful original Hornby Dublo train set which went on the bonfire) when he was bored with them, rather than hand them down for me to enjoy.

Trains always played a major part in our two lives. As small kids, our parents were happy to let us go off by ourselves train-spotting; spending hours on Beckenham Junction station with crowds of other young school be-capped boys writing down the names or numbers of steam engines as they stood clanking, hissing and pouring steam across the platform, or as the diesel pulled express trains to the coast with majestic names like the Bournemouth Belle or the Golden Arrow tore through the station at break neck speed sending our caps flying and filling us with awe.

As small kids, our parents would not have been at all happy to know we had gone off by ourselves playing by the railway at New Beckenham station; the very station where our father caught the morning train to London Bridge. Paul and some similar aged friends, with me in tow, had discovered a derelict house by the station that backed on to the railway line. The house was boarded up, but of course this is purely a magnet to a pack of investigative young boys with rat-like tendencies.

Once we had managed to figure out a way through the 'Danger – No Trespassing' fortifications, and were inside, we discovered the ground floor of the house in a total mess with a litter of broken and burnt furniture, and some very unstable and not to be tested stairs leading to the upstairs rooms, most of which you could see glimpses of through huge holes in the ceiling. There was broken glass everywhere and most window panes had been caved in, but there were still enough for us to enjoy smashing and revelling in that tinkling sound as only naughty boys can. We made noise in waves, with a high pitch of excitement as we broke things, to complete silence as we remembered the house was overlooked by the railway signal-box, and the hugely violent, very shouty, very red-headed signalman who would come and kill us with his giant red-headed axe if he saw or heard us. This house was worth the risk however, it was like no other - it actually had a cave running underneath it - and a dungeon – and a mystery story – and tales of death – and it was haunted! What more could little kids want? Children's TV only lasted an hour a night in those days, computer games were light-years into the future, CCTV had yet to be invented and the Police had bicycles. Only the murderous red axe-man could spoil our fun, and a boy with close-together eyes said he had it on the best authority (having thrown a stone at the signal-box and broken a window) that the red axe-man could run very fast but not for long, so at least most of us would escape if he were to chase us. Not the best news for a round ball, but by this age I was a lot less chubby and the ball mantle had been taken up by my best friend at the time, the wimpy cry-baby called Big Jimmy with the forever snotty nose, bad breath, bad gas, a sister with terrifying hair, and who was only tolerated because his dad owned an ice-cream factory.

Sure enough once we cleared away the debris from a blackened door that led off the downstairs hall, there were some rubbish-strewn steps down to what appeared to be a cave-working carved out of the bedrock. This had roughly hewn walls, a broken and uneven floor, and was just tall enough for the bigger boys to stand up in. The floor was also littered with thousands of bank cheques, all used, and all showing fantastic monetary amounts beyond our avaricious dreams. We of course believed these were the equivalent of cash, which meant we were fabulously rich on one hand, but on the other, liable to be killed by the robber pirate band who must really live here and whose treasure this surely was, and who might come back any minute. We were all scared to pick them up and pocket any at this stage, especially as the close-eyed boy had become 'the font of all knowledge', and stated that if the pirate band caught us with any cheques we would be buried alive along with all the other kids they had killed over the years, which was why there were cave workings in the first place. This of course made perfect sense.

After a few yards the passage was blocked where some of the roof had fallen in, but through a hole in the debris, we could see that the passage continued for what seemed forever. There was nothing for it, we needed to go on and therefore we needed help.

Looking back I have to pinch myself to remember this actually happened.

Three nights later we had eight kids lined up, tooled up, and ready to help dig ourselves to a treasure-trove. It was late evening and past all our bedtimes. All of us without exception had crept silently out of our houses, mostly through bedroom windows, leaving the obligatory football and pillow dreaming away under the bedclothes. We made our way by torchlight to our point of rendezvous, pledging ourselves to our leader - my brother. Of the new contingent I was one of the youngest at seven years of age; the average age was eight. We were all boys except one girl who was pretending to be a boy, with her long blonde hair tucked under a school cap. Somehow even at that age we knew better than to challenge her.

It took ages to get us all quietly into the house through the broken fencing, rusted corrugated iron and nail-ridden posts, but eventually we were all assembled by the blackened door feeling suitably terrified and excited and ready to descend the steps into the passage of mystery. All except Big Jimmy who was blubbing, had already wet himself and wanted to go home, and who was therefore given a stern talking to by my brother. Us younger ones weren't allowed to see what was happening, but we could hear shrieks and whimpers as he was convinced of the error of his ways, and we were assured by the 'font of all knowledge' that it was for his own good.

Paul and I had first come across this strange close-eyed boy when he threw sticks and stones at us from behind a tree whilst we were walking in the local park; it was probably just his quaint way of introducing himself. We threw them back of course and this missile exchange continued until one particularly large stick he picked up stuck to his hand, became horribly gooey, and turned out to be freshly laid dogs' muck. Most people would be horrified by this and rub the worst of the mess off on the grass, but the boy simply wiped his sticky brown hand on his own jacket and trousers, and then ran towards us with a maniac grin on his face and holding out his reeking hand before him, threatening all the while to wipe the residue in our hair. Incidents like this possibly helped me become one of the fastest runners in my school age group.

The second time we encountered the now nicknamed 'dog-dirt kid', Paul and I were train-spotting on Beckenham Junction station when as if from nowhere, the dog-dirt kid sidled up to us and told us he had three return train tickets to London Victoria station if we dared join him for an adventure. This sounded most exciting, especially as our parents would have been horrified to think we were travelling to strange places by train without their knowledge, and especially as all the wonderful express trains we so worshipped terminated at Victoria and so might be there for us to marvel at; so we agreed to go with him. Once aboard the train however, it turned out he had been lying; he didn't have any tickets at all, but he knew how we could get through the ticket barrier at the other end without paying which was a good thing as we had no more than a shilling between us. His plan was to identify a friendly looking old lady on the train and offer to help carry her shopping when we got to Victoria. This way the ticket man would hopefully think we were her grandchildren, and overlook us as we collectively shuffled through the barrier smiling up at and chatting to 'granny', and his scheme worked a treat. A similar ruse, attaching ourselves to a young mother who suddenly found she had three additional children also managed to get us into the News Theatre without paying. This unusual theatre was housed in an Art Deco edifice dating back to before the war years, situated next to the platform where the Golden Arrow was scheduled to depart, and ran a half hour show of mainly 'Tom and Jerry' cartoons interspersed with news headlines to amuse passengers waiting to journey to the romantic French Continent. (Incidentally, the building is still there and can just be seen beneath the advertising banners for a foreign exchange outlet, and if you want to enjoy 'Golden Arrow' luxury, some of the actual Pullman coaches are now preserved on the Bluebell Railway in east Sussex). As we settled ourselves in the plush maroon velvet seats, somewhat wondering how we had managed to end up in central London with a boy we had previously only known by sight, the dog-dirt kid left us on our own for a few minutes, only to return bearing a ketchup and mustard smothered hot dog for each of us and a large cardboard cup of Pepsi-Cola.

'The man in charge of the food counter is a friend of mine' said the boy. 'If you give me all the money you have, I will see what else he has.' And so stripping us of our few pennies he vanished again, but this time coming back with a further two hot dogs and a drink each and an enormous box of popcorn! We were dumbfounded. It was only when we were leaving the theatre I noticed that no-one seemed to be running the hot dog stand, and although it was all switched on, it had been pushed down a small corridor out of sight of the lady on the ticket counter.

By now we were prepared to follow our new friend anywhere, and managing the return journey to Beckenham Junction without any money (we felt like experts at the old lady trick by this stage), we accepted his invitation back to his house for tea, as he lived in a flat above a music shop conveniently situated just across the road from the station.

It was like walking into Ali Baba's den without having to say 'open sesame'. Everywhere we looked were half opened boxes of toys, radios, electrical gadgets, books, clothing and other items you would only expect to find on a busy market stall; there wasn't even any space to sit down. We instinctively knew something was not quite right, but we daren't say anything especially as the boy had a very shifty looking close-eyed Dad who sidled in from the kitchen to greet us, and I know I felt very guilty accepting one of the fancy cakes he offered me, as if I was somehow stealing something.

'Do you want to see what Dad has got me for Christmas?' said the excited boy, and we all three followed him into the front room where a very large object was concealed beneath a white sheet. As the boy pulled the cloth back we were amazed to see revealed a huge sparkly red and silver drum kit, complete with a stool, drumsticks and two sets of symbols.

'It's taken Dad three months to steal this piece by piece from the shop downstairs.' said the beaming dog-dirt kid, pointing at his father who glowed with embarrassed pride and smiled fondly at his son. 'One day when he's managed to get me the electric guitar and amplifier I've got my eye on, I'm going to start my own pop group!'

Now here he was again in his new guise, and busily taking money off the new kids as an entrance fee to join the 'Gold Rush'.

Even at such a young age we must have all seen *The Great Escape* for sure enough within minutes we had an impressive tunnelling technique in place with kids at the front taking it in turns to pass back rock and soil to other kids, who threw this out into the main room downstairs. No-one worked harder than the blonde school cap who by this time I was in love with and determined to save if anything untoward should happen. Within no more than half an hour we had a big enough space to crawl through to see where the passage went. Although I wasn't at the front, from the 'oohs' and 'aahs' this must have been what it was like for Howard Carter when he first broke into Tutankhamen's treasure chamber with his lordly mates.

We took it in turns to wriggle through the gap and into the passage beyond, becoming increasingly aware of the fact that if we had to retreat it was going to be hard on the boys leading the way. It is therefore of no surprise that the 'font of all knowledge' and my brother pushed us smaller kids forward at this stage to the point where I was the leading pioneer, holding tightly the hand of the blonde school cap, and thus feeling immensely courageous.

The passage went forward for about twenty yards and then mysteriously emerged into a sunken greenhouse of immense proportions in the back garden of the house. Most of the glass of this mighty edifice was still somehow intact (at this stage), but the building was bereft of plants. A central path led to some steps up to ground level and to the middle of a terrace next to what would once have been a lawn.

Having gone to so much trouble to be here at such a late hour and at the risk of so much punishment, we were naturally a little disappointed not to be in the midst of glistening statues of gold, bars of silver and chests brimming with jewels; especially a pretty shiny necklace and a gem-studded tiara to adorn the blonde school cap.

Emerging onto the terrace, we stood around a small pond that had caught our collective attention. Despite the Moon and the frail glow from the signal-box casting their light on the waters of this small, shining but pitch black body of water, there was something about this pond that did not feel right. For one, it seemed bottomless, and as we rimmed its perimeter it was almost as if it was sucking us down to join some demonic water babies already within. Secondly, it was so calm we all stood mesmerised and motionless, forgot our treasure hunting, and in total silence peered deeply down. Now it was time for the 'font of all knowledge' with his narrow eyes glinting in the moonlight, and the cool night air making us gather ever closer and shudder together - to tell us a story.

'Many years ago' he said, looking round and piercing our very souls with his gaze. 'There lived a kindly family here with a beautiful lady, twin children, a blonde boy and blonde girl who were devoted to each other' (a little hand squeezes mine), 'and a caring father who went to war as someone in the Navy. When he got home one leave he got into dealing with some bad men who made him do bad things, and so his wife was going to leave him and take the children from him. He couldn't take this and got very violent, smashing things and thundering around. The little children were so scared they ran into the garden and fell into this pool.' We all take a step back. 'Unfortunately the little children were too small and couldn't swim. Although they cried out the father was making so much noise in the house they couldn't be heard and were slowly sucked down by the strangling weeds which tentacled up from the depths – and after a short while all that could be seen in the black waters were a few bubbles as their short lives were squeezed from them'. (There are tears from the owner of the little hand, so I put a caring arm around her).

We all stare ever harder at the pit before us and I am sure most imagine those tiny hands beckoning upwards, and the haunted baby faces as they sink ever further away from the angels above them; their short memories playing their short lives back to them before they are slowly and painfully extinguished as if a match flame.

'The father realising he was out of control, looks for the children and seeing no sign of them approaches this pool. All he can see are the remains of the bubbles and splashes of water around the edge of the pool from their futile struggles. He dives in and dives down, but he too is caught by the strangling weed and dies the same slow tortuous death as his dear little twins. All this happened many, many years ago and no-one knows what happened to the mother, but no-one has ever lived here since, and sometimes it is said, late at night, you can hear her crying for her loved ones.' So ends his tale – he looks around to gauge our reactions and nods sagely.

Thank-you so very much 'font of all knowledge'! Half the kids are crying; Big Jimmy has messed his pants big time; and at a signal from Paul we all tear like mad back the way we have come to escape the House of Death. This of course takes time because we have to climb through the debris; we are all fighting not to be last; and of course as always happens when you are in a massive hurry and can't make any headway, someone at the back shouts 'I can hear someone coming behind us, it must be the red axe-man!' Arrgghhhhhh!!!.

Eventually we make it back through the black door and are standing, shaking, in the main room of the house; breathing heavily and feeling very scared but also angry with the close-eyed boy for telling such a story. In fact he does receive a couple of well aimed blows from another of the bigger boys for ruining things, as we are all far too terrified to go back down the tunnel and explore further.

Paul decides we must all calm down, make sure we have everything with us and agree not to take away any of the cheques just in case the pirate gang come after us. We must of course all promise not to tell anyone where we have been, what we have been doing, or who we have been with or we will be killed, buried and eaten, all in that unlikely order. By now we were quiet, we were more tired than we had ever been in our lives and we wanted to go home. Then I remember a glimmering light entering the room. Not a bright light but a similar light to that from our dim torches, although this light was not at the end of any beam we were shining.

We all saw the light and looked from it to each other in a quizzical way. An initial fear I had was that it was from the red axe-man finally come to get us, but there was no sound of heavy boots stamping towards us and we were making no noise above our own breathing. It was too quiet (a very small, very cold hand clenched mine and nails dug into my flesh). The light mesmerised us all as we watched it slowly move up the unsafe staircase where none of us had dared to tread, then show itself periodically through holes in the ceiling from the floor above, then become immensely bright, shining out from some unseen room above. I recall the air becoming very heavy and cloying and myself feeling a little giddy (the little hand was shaking and I could smell fear). Somehow the 'font of all knowledge' had summoned up the courage to follow the light, and we all held our breath as he slowly and carefully risked each creaking and shaking stair and made his way upstairs. Most of us only dared peer through our fingers as he reached the corner of the stairs where the banister had fallen away, and the boards shook as he slowly stole ever upwards with nothing to hold on to. Finally he reached the landing and disappeared after the light. Moments later there came the unmistakable sound of a piano playing from upstairs, getting steadily louder. It sounded quite beautiful and we looked at each other thinking this could not possibly be the close-eyed kid playing. Then suddenly the playing stopped and the boy appeared at the top of the stairs. It was like seeing a ghost. His face was ashen and his close-knitted eyes were like dark pits, but most shocking of all was his hair; it had turned completely white. He stood motionless and staring straight ahead of him, as if in a stupor. Paul was about to call to him when the piano started playing again.

We ran hell for leather from that house, never to return, and for some strange inexplicable reason, never to discuss it amongst ourselves ever again. I don't remember what happened to the boy, we never saw him again. I don't even remember escaping through the fencing and other barriers. I have no recollection of what happened to the little hand or even who she was. I just remember running and running and not wanting to be the last out of that house, and not daring to look round and being too scared to cry; and all the time feeling an icy finger creeping steadily up my spine...

I am on the late train this morning, often referred to as the 'Director's Special', as by the time it arrives into London Bridge, only a Director could get away with being so late for work. This train also has the advantage of having larger tables, each with four seats, so I can study in comfort. At this time of day the train is generally not that busy, all the business commuters having long gone; however the off-peak fare does attract hives of women passengers buzzing off to London's West End for a shopping and luncheon extravaganza. I seem to act as a kind of large, nectar-rich flower on such days, as the ladies seem to enjoy swarming around me as I try and concentrate on my studies; talking at each other as loudly as possible, and of course taking absolutely no notice of what each other is saying. They also insist on having their showy handbags on the table in front of them, within which they constantly delve *Mary Poppins*-style, bringing to the surface to utilise or enjoy: food items; a phone; another older-model phone; make up (especially compacts dustily spilling their contents); pictures of children or grandchildren or a dog; more food items of a chocolate nature; and always a large book or magazine which takes up loads of space, and which they have no intention of reading. All of this makes it extremely hard to reserve my tiny little piece of table for my really very small text book. If I am really unlucky, a lady with a greater surface area than is deemed clinically prudent will have squeezed in next to me, and during the course of the journey will slowly but deliberately, spread her rosette leaves over me in a daisy-like fashion as if I was a lawn. If I dare to make eye contact, trying to mentally infuse the word 'hush' (or something altogether less polite) into their thought patterns, they smile sweetly and carry-on regardless; or worse, ask 'what are you reading dear?', then when I reply, exclaim 'Ooh! It must be hard to study with us talking so much!', then giggle, smile sweetly and carry-on regardless.

Today's topic is **Energy**, something which we are told cannot be created or destroyed, and consequently a subject requiring deep thought and very hard to get your head around, especially with any distraction. As the ladies have indeed spotted me and are making a beeline in my direction, I plonk a digit into each ear, sink into my seat, close my eyes, resign myself to a wasted journey, and think about days before carriages were so open plan…

A VERY NAUGHTY BOY

It was at age eight when I first started commuting. Unfortunately the age of steam had died, so my first 'regular' train was an electrically driven set of carriages with no discernible engine, running from the South London station of Hayes to London Bridge. A very boring type of train at the time compared to the hissing, smoking, steaming giants I had wished for, but nevertheless now looked back upon with nostalgia.

These trains were new and very posh. The Southern Region livery was a lovely green colour with creamy yellow writing, and the inside of the carriages

was all cream melamine walls with heavily varnished woodwork and plush seats. They even had nicely framed pictures advertising wonderful English resorts you could visit by train.

Every morning the carriages were adorned with posh gentlemen. Their livery was mostly pinstriped of the waist-coated variety, white shirts with separate starched white collars which had to be painfully pinned on, and a dark sombre tie with the ever faithful Windsor knot. A very few gentlemen dared to venture to wear a brightly coloured bow tie as part of their outfit, but these individuals were considered 'different', even by the young children, and rightly avoided. Without exception all the gentlemen would have placed on the brand new netting racks above their seats; a leather briefcase with their initials stencilled in gold, a tightly wound umbrella and a bowler hat. Their annoyingly large broadsheet newspapers which they were handed by the bowing, scraping individual from the newsagents as they passed through the booking-hall and took their daily obsequious dose from the ticket-master, would be on their laps waiting to intrude on their neighbour's space, which was naturally limited as these new carriages were split into compact compartments. Every carriage had six compartments each consisting of eight seats – four per side without any seat arms, and with no interconnecting corridor in the carriage. It was obviously therefore imperative on such an essential introduction to the busy working day that you always had the same seat; in the same compartment; in the same carriage; on the same train; at the same strict railway time; and with the same

fellow commuters none of whom you knew, would ever want to converse with, would ever want to know in a personal capacity, but would miss as much as a lost limb if ever they failed to be in their allotted place – such was, and such is commuting!

My first commute – Outward. Enter a schoolboy! It is his first day at Prep' School. He also has his own livery; a smart new black blazer complete with badge and mystery Latin motto; grey shorts; a white shirt and neatly knotted blue tie; long grey socks with black tops emerging from shiny black shoes (with laces); a brown leather satchel; a shilling for 'tuck', and a large sized cap as his head is already oversized and round and so unlikely to grow to any significant extent over the next four or five years. He gets on at New Beckenham station and is only going two stops to Catford Bridge where his new posh public school awaits to ensnare him.

He does not know the commuting rules. He is respectful of his elders and he wants to please. But there is nowhere to sit, nor is there anywhere convenient to stand as highly polished shoes at the end of pin-striped legs occupy all the no-mans land between the two sides of the compartment. He somehow manages to struggle in, all the while being buffeted by growling and muttering men behind their papers. Finally he stands like someone unwillingly deformed between a sea of deliberately unhelpful legs, and hangs on to the overhead netting he can barely reach, and wonders if this is his life as a commuter forever more.

My first commute – Return. The schoolboy's livery has lost some of the 'showroom' finish it enjoyed in the morning. His parents had made doubly sure in advance that he knew the route from Catford Bridge station to the school, and that he would be safe crossing two busy road junctions by himself. What they had not warned him of was the gauntlet of 'Council School' kids he would have to run, all of whom had an in-bred dislike for poncey public school boys, especially those on their inaugural day and hence unaccompanied by similarly attired but elder 'knights in armour'. The shiny black shoes are thoroughly scuffed, a lace is broken; the socks hang limply around his ankles as if in despair; the shorts and blazer have gained a camouflage pattern consisting principally of dust, mud and an undisclosed toxic substance; the blue tie has been given a much tighter knot by a 'big boy' who personally revels in choking all newcomers and will have to be removed with scissors; and the cap was lost within the first three seconds. The schoolboy's bodywork is relatively unscathed however, so despite his somewhat tyrannical Form-teacher having given him a detention and a blow to the head for turning up dishevelled on his first day, he has been in fine spirits. These have been particularly lifted by the new sights, sounds, routine and playmates that will become a major ingredient of his life for what to him seems to be forevermore. Nevertheless, the schoolboy has had ample time to reflect upon the nasty, suited, booted, bowler-hat headed fellow travellers that tried to spoke his new adventure. He has also enjoyed a journey home in the exact same compartment, in company with an irresistible large thick-tipped indelible black felt pen he found on

Teacher's desk when 'Sir' was outside the classroom unfairly abusing another boy for feeling sick. He has had the compartment otherwise to himself. He has been able to wipe his very dirty shoes on the starched white headrests. He has bounced up and down on the plush seats and run ecstatically backwards and forwards from door to door. He has hung his head out of the window and screamed with delight at the World because he is only eight years old, and he has climbed up and lain comfortably in the nets above the seats as if he was a lost boy on a cruise with Captain Hook. What joy! What fun it is to be trusted to be on a brand new fast-moving electric train all by yourself, at such a young age. What freedom!

Oh dear, oh dear!

The irresistible large thick-tipped indelible black felt pen has been whispering to the schoolboy as he day dreams in his imaginary hammock, and suggesting revengeful mischief. It is not his doing, he is a good boy, his parents trust him. But the pen suggests he write names above each of the seats with an arrow pointing to the intended occupant on the morrow. Oh dear indeed! What a naughty pen!

My second commute – Outward. The schoolboy makes sure he gets into the same compartment as the day before and does the same balancing act between the unhelpful pin-striped legs. He deliberately stares at his feet, far too scared to look at the compartment walls for fear he would give himself away. Eventually however he peeks at the posh gentlemen in turn, none of whom seem to be reading their papers today. The large man in the corner unknowingly labelled 'Bogey', is sitting opposite 'Pansy' and trying not to snigger as Pansy is a very stern looking gentleman but coincidentally wearing a yellow-ochre bow-tie. It is obvious from his violent expression that Pansy is less than impressed with the labelling of his fellow commuters, neither is 'Idiot' next to him who is sitting opposite 'Wet Pants'. 'Dunce' is another gentleman trying not to grin too widely as he stares at his opposite number 'Farty', who is in turn grinning at Dunce's label and that of 'Weed' next to him, who of all those in the compartment is most aptly labelled, he being a diminutive man in an ill fitting suit and a much too thin tie; wearing thick glasses and huddled against the carriage wall as if for protection from the rest of the occupants. Weed is timidly perched opposite the final member of the named contingent who has the dubious honour of having been given the only rude word the schoolboy knew at this age - 'Bugger'.

It is plainly obvious after a short while that for one thing they would like to discuss the horror of having to sit underneath the names with each other, but as they have never spoken, no-one is so bold or common enough to commence proceedings. But most of all you can tell from the way they glance upwards, showing the whites of their eyes as if they could see through the backs of their skulls, they are desperate to know what their own label is. This is especially so if they suspect the gentlemen opposite are beginning to grin and nod to each other in a knowing sort of way. The only way to find out, of course, is to physically turn round and thus give away the fact the whole situation bothers them in the slightest.

In the event, no-one does look round whilst I am still aboard, but as I struggle through the pin-stripy bracken to alight at my stop I receive three distinct kicks on the back of the legs, the last of which is from the Weed, who even tries to trip me onto the track between the train and the platform to an early death. Needless to say I never travel in that compartment again. Needless to say I keep the naughty pen safely hidden away, and needless to say, I do play the naming game again many years later; but this time with fellow pupils and when my imagination is able to express itself through a suitably enhanced vocabulary.

It is evening, dark outside, and I am on a late train home from the City. The carriage is virtually empty and it is November 5th. In the United Kingdom that means countless families will be enjoying firework displays, standing around bonfires, and burning stuffed pyjamas representing that bad man Guido Fawkes who tried to blow up the King of England four hundred years ago. We still like to scare our children to sleep with horror stories of how Guy was hung, drawn, and quartered and what a grisly death he suffered; but in reality he simply fell off the scaffold and broke his neck, thereby missing out on all the niceties in store for him. These days, many people replace Guy with effigies of Bin Laden; a preacher of hate – especially the nasty one with the hooked hand, the incumbent Prime Minister; a fallen celebrity; or other unpopular individuals.

Quite deliberately, I have spent my Firework Night commute reading a text book on rocket technology and the early space programme. I already knew the Nazis were ahead of the game with their V2 rocket in the Second World War, and I also knew that the Russians were the first to orbit Planet Earth with Sputnik, because that happened in the same year I was born. But I didn't know that they were also the first to land an object on the Moon, ten years before the American Apollo missions. One day I would really like to attend a rocket launch which is supposed to be awesome, and tonight it would at least be nice to see some firework substitutes shoot up into the night sky. Frustratingly I won't be able to enjoy watching anything, because modern day trains have been deliberately designed to ruin your evenings viewing. Air conditioning means you can no longer open a window to hang your head outside, which in any event would be deemed childish and irresponsible, and the overhead strip lighting is designed not to be tampered with. So the starkly lit carriage interior allows nothing more thrilling than your own moody, ghostly reflection in the window. It was fortunately not always the case…

DANGER UXB

I have always enjoyed that special time of year when fireworks finally go on sale. The weather is cold and fresh; the autumn evenings are long with dusk setting in shortly after tea-time; there are still some conkers on the trees or hiding in their shells amidst the camouflage of leaves underneath; Christmas is only a few short weeks away; and the sweetshops are full of colourful posters of dastardly Guy Fawkes being lit up by rockets and explosions, or being burnt to death on a huge bonfire. Inside the shops themselves, in addition to the familiar aroma of candy and liquorice, there is the additional smell of egg-box cardboard when you try on one of the coloured Guy Fawkes masks, and the unmistakable aroma of gunpowder and cordite emanating from the locked glass cabinet - the magical cabinet where the fireworks themselves, in all their wonderful shapes and colours, are kept away from eager young hands.

Obviously we were forbidden to take fireworks to school, but the afternoons and weekends would invariably find my jacket or blazer pockets full of the smaller ones the shopkeepers would happily sell to tiny children. One pocket would hold a box of bangers (twelve sticks that looked like dynamite and were considered so precious they were to be used sparingly); another pocket would harbour some jumping jacks to be thrown at people; my top pocket would hide a box of matches (always the red-tipped strike anywhere kind); and my inside zip pocket would play host to my most treasured accompaniment – a round metal tin of Jetex fuse wire. This wonderful material could be bought in the local 'toy and model' shop along with solid fuel capsules to power miniature Jetex rocket engines. These were in turn used to drive wonderful toys such as the Bluebird car or Bluebird seaplane, of Donald Campbell record-breaking fame. The fuse wire wasn't supposed to be used for anything other than with the Jetex brand toys of course, but the Saturday morning 'slightly dippy' assistant in our toyshop was oblivious to this and so blithely sold my brother and I copious quantities to be put to good misuse. The one item my parents never allowed me to have on my person, unless my highly responsible elder brother was with me, was petrol - after all, I was not yet eight years of age. If I was out having fun with him and his friends however, I was allowed to take a tin of cigarette lighter fuel with me, and on special occasions (if my parents had gone out for the day taking my two year old baby brother Timmy with them, and leaving us completely to our own devices), I could take my turn proudly carrying my father's nice bright red can of lawnmower petrol. If anyone had thought to throw a black sheet over me I could have easily been an early role model for many a would-be martyr.

Incidentally, we were only ever stopped once by the Police for carrying petrol, this was by a sergeant on a bicycle when I was unfortunately in charge of the can. When sternly asked 'What I was doing with it, Sonny', I was naturally struck dumb and frozen to the spot at having been addressed by such a scary and angry looking pillar of authority. He didn't seem any happier either when my brother explained we were looking after it for our dad in case it was stolen, and the policeman insisted we pour it down a nearby drain. He ignored our plaintive cries of 'angry father', 'loss of pocket money' and similarly feeble arguments, instead threatening us with a good hiding; but then this was the sixties. If that happened now in the 21st century, we could argue about damaging the environment by polluting an important water course; that flammable substances can only be disposed of in designated areas etc.; and probably report him and have him sacked and fined for insisting we break countless regulations, using violent language, and causing us undue stress. We could probably even Google a good 'no cure no pay' lawyer on our mobile phones, while we smile nonchalantly at the good Sergeant knowing we have the future of his career in our hands.

What my parents thought we were doing with this 'Junior Arson Set' I don't know, but I suspect my mother thought we were up to no good - although as we ourselves never suffered any burns she turned a blind eye. A couple of years later she even knitted us and my brother's friends some black IRA-style balaclavas, 'to keep you nice and warm whilst you are playing outside, oh - and so the neighbours don't recognise you'.

Father did once help us have some fun with Jetex fuse. Mum was busy with new born baby Timmy and so Dad would take Paul and me to nearby Keston Ponds on a Saturday morning to sail toy boats. I had a tiny red boat on a string tied to my wrist so I couldn't lose it, and Paul had a bright yellow yacht with a two foot mast which would race across the pond from one side to the other. The yacht was at the mercy of the wind of course, and so sometimes would get caught up with one or other of the many radio-controlled model boats cruising the waters, angering their anorak-clad, mostly adult owners, a couple of whom even wore 'Captain' hats and sported white beards! It was of little surprise to me therefore to find one Friday tea-time Paul and Dad sitting together at the kitchen table working feverishly over some alterations to the yellow yacht, which Paul had by then become bored with sailing. Much Plasticine, petrol, Jetex fuse wire and plastic model paint later, they had created a heavily disguised 'Bomb Vessel' to be launched on its final voyage the next morning.

The idea was that the little yacht would reach the centre of the boating pond and simply explode, shocking everyone, especially the Captain Birdseye brigade, and giving us a great laugh. Instead, at the same time we launched the yacht, someone had set off their enormous grey motorised model battleship on a converging path. This leviathan must have been five feet in length; have taken months if not years to create; was festooned with gun turrets; and even had a working model helicopter aboard. Within minutes the two vessels collided, some of the rigging from the yacht got caught up in the superstructure of the mini naval masterpiece, and the three of us could be seen running away like mad.

The owner of the battleship was kindly bringing his craft back to the edge of the pond to release our yacht, when from a distant vantage point we could see not an explosion, but a small flame appear on the deck of the yacht. What we had created was not a bomb vessel at all, but something the ancient Greeks and Sir Francis Drake used to great effect; a Fireship. We watched just long enough to see the warship become a ball of flame before I was picked up by Dad who dragged Paul with him to the car, and we drove off in a cloud of dust.

Needless to say we didn't dare go back to the ponds for a very long time.

Now; most kids would be happy with being bought a box of fireworks, following the safety instructions and watching an adult put on a small but enjoyable display in the garden. These days in fact, most children probably get no nearer to fireworks than at an organised display. Instead, we created a veritable firework factory in my brother's bedroom. We and his friends would pool our fireworks and set to work with abandon. First we would open up all the rockets and create newer, larger rockets using toilet roll holders wrapped in sticky-tape and longer balsawood sticks, packing in loads of gunpowder and star-shell pellets. Some of these would in turn be tied to large aerial bomb fireworks with a view to the latter firework being ignited by the sparks from the rocket on its way up, and thus exploding when the stick returned it to the ground. The fun of these was that you never knew where they would land until you heard the bangs, and hopefully the sound of breaking glass or screams. Other large rockets would have a smaller rocket tied to them but upside down. The principle here was that by the time the large rocket had reached its zenith, the smaller rocket would have become lit from the sparks, and the whole thing would then return to Earth at very high speed. These were extremely unpredictable in flight, and many a time we had to lay flat as the rockets rose no more than a few feet, turned towards us, and then careered in our direction. Most of the other, less interesting fireworks would then be set into holes in a cardboard box, and connected together using Jetex fuse-wire so that they all went off pretty well simultaneously, giving a somewhat brief but spectacular display. Not only us, but most parents equally enjoyed watching us put on these events as long as their own houses were not in the immediate target area. Hence, not all parents were invited.

When I was first commuting to school, the train journey home was only a short one and I was home in time for tea well before it was dark enough for a firework party. By the time I was a teenager, I was still at the same school but we had moved to Chipstead, Surrey, and I had at least a one hour train journey each way (which went via London Bridge), as well as a much longer school day. By the time I was travelling home on Firework Night therefore, it was already dark outside and the youngest kids were having their early displays in their gardens as the train rattled past on the embankments. The problem was, the carriage lights made it almost impossible to see anything clearly through the glass other than your own reflection, and cast a glare if you had the window open, which also let in the freezing air. The simplest solution was to remove the light-bulbs in your compartment. You now had a dark cosy box from which to observe the myriad of firework displays and bonfires as the train carried you home to your own waiting box of explosive delight. These light-bulbs being of a specific railway voltage and therefore of no use to anyone else, had the additional advantage of becoming ammunition to throw at those quaint little railway workers huts thoughtfully provided every half mile or so. The bulbs also made a wonderful inwardly popping and tinkling sound as they imploded on impact.

This bulb removal habit actually continued until much later in life, in fact until the corridor style trains were eventually replaced. Many a time my brother and I, or even more recently my eldest daughter and I when travelling together; would be standing in either a corridor or the guard's van unable to get a seat in the evening, and we would remove the bulbs; not only to create a view into the darkness outside but to create an ambience. With the train journey doubling up as a chance to have a relaxing aperitif (I have always hated brightly lit bars), it was important to create the correct environment. I found that a darkened corridor or guard's compartment, with pitch darkness outside lit by the occasional spark from the tracks; old fashioned wood surrounds; the rattling noise and the motion of the train; the smell of old polish mixed with grease and oil; the taste of the Sauvignon grape on my palate; and with mini-bottle of the same in my hand, would in my mind create the romantic atmosphere of the salon in one of those wonderful long-distance French express trains, the like of which I had experienced on a long-ago memorable journey from Paris to Marseilles. How nostalgic an atmosphere to encourage good conversation, nurture deep thoughts, and promote close relationships. We would, of course, still 'pop' the bulbs against the conveniently sited little huts.

The most dangerous 'fireworks' we ever played with were some very large marine distress flares, the type used by very large vessels at sea. I had come across a batch of these quite by chance. My school was of the progressive type that thought five days a week insufficient, and insisted on you also attending on a Saturday, but which as a reward allowed Wednesday afternoon free to do either Rugby, Cricket, cross-country running, or some similar such penance if you were either a new boy, or silly enough to turn up. The only other boy from my school who lived anywhere remotely near me and I, neither of us being silly, would leave school on Wednesday lunchtime, travel back to Chipstead station and dig up our bags of 'explorers clothes', which we kept buried in a shallow hole in nearby woods. Exchanging jeans, a camouflage top and commando style hat for our giveaway school uniforms, we would then spend the afternoon 'exploring'. In practice this meant going from garden to garden of some of the biggest houses in the village, not getting caught, and all the time looking for things we could 'discover' and put in the handy sacks we carried with us. On one such adventure I chanced upon the above mentioned flares in an old shed, at the bottom of a very large garden. But, because they looked very dangerous to use, and in any event were some twenty years past their use by date, I hid them in my bedroom at home and forgot all about them. This was until one firework night when for once my father was home early. Dad loved fireworks as much as the rest of us; had been allowed to be in charge for once; and so we were all bitterly disappointed and stood looking lost when our display was finished, and all the fireworks were gone. Suddenly I remembered the flares and within minutes duly handed one over to Dad.

In true form, Dad asked no questions as to where this wonder had materialized from, but read the instructions and the use by date, and sensibly suggested we all stand well back. He then dug a small hole to stand the flare in and struck the ignition paper with the wooden striker that came as part of the packaging. I think the idea of these flares is that they are supposed to be fitted into some sort of metal launching mechanism, and fire off a capsule about 1000 feet into the air which then explodes, launching a ball of burning magnesium which gravity brings back to Earth by parachute. This parachute obviously maximises the time the brightly burning flare can be seen by other vessels beyond the horizon. I expect this is probably what would have happened twenty years previous, and if we had had the proper launcher, and if we had been at sea, and if we had been on a vessel in distress. Instead, our capsule rose just above the trees which bordered our house from the road, and landed with a loud thud in the forecourt of the petrol station opposite, which was fortunately closed for the evening. We looked at each other in expectation and horror. Sure enough a few seconds later there was a loud explosion and the whole petrol station lit up in an incredible bright white and blue as the magnesium ignited. At that stage we should have run – to have a large ball of magnesium burning at 2000° C in the middle of a forecourt above giant tanks of petrol is not a good thing. Instead what galvanized us into action was the voice of the man who ran the Post Office next to the petrol station shouting for someone to call the Police, Fire Brigade and anyone else they could get hold of. We all ran inside the house and hid, and listened.

Mum, Dad, the dog, my two brothers and I were all lying down in the lounge below the ledge of the large window to the front of the house, silent as mice. Thoughtfully Mum had quickly doused all the main house lights when we ran inside. From where we lay, we could see an increasing number of flashing blue lights reflecting into the lounge as more and more emergency service vehicles arrived on the scene. There was the unmistakable sound of fire engines, the slamming of ambulance doors and lots of Police. Then we could hear people in the garden right outside our protective window, someone saying a parachute flare had been found by a fireman, how it must have been dropped from an aircraft in distress, and that Gatwick Airport and Air Traffic Control must be alerted.

Then we heard the bloody Post Office man again (who by the way had a really silly hair-cut), shouting,

'Mr Page, Mr Page, is this anything to do with you? Mr Page', and sure enough within a few seconds he was banging on the front door with some policemen who were shining torches searchingly through the window above our heads. This was a nightmare and we all knew we were going to be in serious trouble. Then we realised Dad had vanished. He had run upstairs and come back down, first putting on the hall light, then opening the front door, rubbing his eyes, and pretending he and the family had been fast asleep, and what was the fuss. Amazingly we heard a policeman explain about the flare, apologise for waking him up and then Dad shutting the door. When he came into the lounge we were stunned to see Dad wearing tightly fitting striped pyjamas *over* his suit, still with his shirt and tie showing and wearing black work shoes! How we got away with it I will never know, after all it was only six in the evening – but the horrid man from the horrid Post Office with the horrid haircut knew, and none of us dared go into his shop and face him for a very long time. Besides which, he wouldn't sell fireworks to kids anyway! Horrid man.

This weekend I have been staying at my home in Rudyard Kipling country, and I am consequently travelling to London on the train which comes up from Hastings, of invasion fame. I take this route quite often, coupling up with a fellow work colleague who joins the train at the spa town of Tunbridge Wells, and who will happily fall asleep whilst I study away as usual, but not until we have passed the next stop – High Brooms. This appropriately named habitation is home to a coven of young witches who always catch our train and always sit in the same carriage as us. They are classed as witches for the simple reasons that they cackle loudly; they wear excessive amounts of make-up giving them a Macbethian sinister look; they always seem to be plotting against someone or other (from the snippets of conversation that we strain to overhear); and they point fingers, sneer, and make snide remarks about the strange classically-attired girl who always flaunts majestically down the central aisle half way through the journey as if she was queen of the cat-walk. You can see why we don't just change carriage, and always stay alert for this entertainment.

Thinking of witches and the supernatural actually fits well with my current topic - quantum theory; the realm of the likes of Professor Stephen

Hawking. This describes a world we can't and will never see; where the laws of physics are very different from those we experience at our 'macro-level'; where our Universe might just be a bubble in an infinite world of bubbles; and where despite the fact that Einstein said we can't travel faster than light (which somewhat negates the possibility of time travel); every tiny electron, inside every tiny atom; knows what every other electron in the Universe is doing; and all at the same time! Which when you consider that the distances involved are billions of light years, is quite fantastical. I find it hard enough to accept that an electron inside my body knows what an electron inside a tree I can see outside my window is doing! I'm sure if our High Brooms witches brought aboard a Ouija board, they too could conjure up improbable whimsies from a world just as mysterious as the quantum one – if you believe in that sort of thing…

I very deliberately, slowly and soundlessly squatted down on the carpet at the staircase end of the upstairs landing; I was next to the door to my bedroom which was off an L-shape at the top of the stairs. His room was at the other end of the landing and his door was closed, as it had been for the past few months; but I knew he was in his room. There was a banister at the top of the stairs and squatting where I was I could view

56

between two of the balusters and so feel they were acting as a kind of shield, fielding my view between them. There were three other doors leading off the landing; my parents' room was on the left hand side, but they were away, as always. But I knew he was in his room.

My father was Financial Chairman of the World's largest insurance broker and spent nearly all his time buying up other insurance brokers across the globe, and my Mother always travelled with him - now. This time they were in Bermuda.

On the right hand side of the landing was my elder brother Paul's bedroom, which of course no one was allowed in – ever, even though he now worked in Baltimore, also in insurance, and would soon be getting married to a nice American girl. Next to Paul's room was a small box room with just sufficient space for a bed, and which was the room we moved my younger brother into when he became too terrified to stay in his own room, and when his screaming became too unbearable. His own room was the room at the far end of the landing, with the door shut. But the light was on; I could see a shaft of light between the bottom of the door and the landing carpet, and I **knew** he was in his room.

It had been dark outside when I had got home. Even though I was only sixteen, most evenings I would take my wonderful golden retriever, Thunder, for a long walk up to a cosy pub at the top of the village, and there I would play darts in the public bar with some elderly men and drink a couple of pints of beer. Thunder obviously hated anything as common as darts and so would spend his time in the posh saloon bar, shaking hands with the locals; drinking anything people were foolish enough to leave within his reach; then urinating against the counter. There had been times when I had to beg a lift home for us both, because Thunder was either unwilling or too insensible to walk more than a few steps, and certainly would have been incapable of the mile or so trek downhill.

The house had felt different when we returned this time. It was a modern house built for my parents a few years before by a Mr. Clegg, a Jehovah's Witness. I remember we had to turn the radio off whenever he came to fix or finish off anything. Mother had given the house the deplorable name of 'Vanity House' because she had so many mirrors everywhere. They even had a sign made and stuck it ostentatiously in the front garden until I set fire to it one night, and blamed the arson on another kid in the village. The house stood on a corner plot in a nice large garden separated into four lawns, myself being responsible for doing the mowing and leaf sweeping, in return for much needed beer money. The road we were in was still unmade, just stones and gravel, and it abutted a lane across which was a short road leading past a proud parade of shops to the local train station; from where I would catch the 7.52 to London Bridge, on the way to my school in Catford, South London. The lane itself was supposedly quiet, but very busy in the brief morning and evening rush hours, as drivers used it as a cut through to avoid the massive roadworks taking place to build what became the London Orbital Motorway. Sometimes it could take what seemed like forever to cross the lane, but they never put in a pedestrian crossing, even after my accident.

It was during the power cuts when I was knocked down. The miners' strike had been going on for weeks and the government had introduced restrictions on power availability due to a shortage of coal. My mother's mum, our Nana, was the first casualty in our family. She lived alone in Leicester in a typical pre-war terraced house, but with a railway at the bottom of the garden and a gasworks opposite. She used to thrill us with stories of German bombers circling overhead, trying to blow up the gasworks whilst she continued hanging out the washing as if nothing was happening. If the Germans had ever managed a direct hit, her little house would have been part of a very large crater, and you wouldn't be reading this story. Her house was the type with a very steep flight of steps leading to the upstairs rooms, and she was on the top step about to come down when the power-cut did make a direct hit; the lights went out, and she fell. She died a few days later in Leicester Infirmary. (I had always thought that an infirmary sounded like the sort of place where you ended your days. Even the dictionary describes 'infirmary' as a place for the sick and aged, whereas at least a 'hospital' has the more positive spin of being a place to nurse and cure.)

It was winter-time and very dark when I was trying to cross the lane to our house. I was on the way home from school; it took me two hours to commute so it was in the middle of rush hour. The traffic was more intense than usual because no traffic lights were working on the major routes, which were consequently snarled up. There were also no streetlamps or house lights working, and so apart from the seemingly endless snaking car head and tail lights, everywhere was gloom. If you ever see a gap in the traffic and decide to cross the road half-way, don't! I was hit by a car with no lights on. I never saw the car and I assume they never saw me because they certainly didn't stop. I know it was a red car though because the back of my grey school jumper was completely red where the paint had scraped off during the impact.

I don't know how long I was unconscious, but when I came round there was a crowd of people standing over me, including two ancient sisters who lived up the road in a strange house with a turret and no electricity; and who were praying for me. They all thought I was dying because there was so much blood coming out of my mouth, but luckily this was not internal, and only due to my having landed on my face which had become something you didn't want to see in a mirror. No-one could get near me either, as Thunder had naturally taken complete control of the situation; was lying on top of me; and licking up the blood in between bouts of barking and growling at anyone who tried to interfere. It was a fortunate thing I wasn't dying, as it took over an hour for an ambulance to be able to get to me, and another two hours to find a hospital that had power and could take a casualty. As may be imagined, my mother was not one of those that Christmas who put together a food parcel for the striking miners' families.

Now here was Thunder, crouching next to me at the top of the stairs, and we **both** knew he was in his room.

It is amazing just how many thoughts and emotions can flow through you in literally sub-seconds. The light is on in his room. Did I put it on? No, I never go in there. Could Mum and Dad be back? No of course not, their car is not in the garage and anyway they are not due back for days yet. Could it be burglars? No, why would they go in there; there is nothing other than his clothes and toys, left just as they were the day he was killed. Why am I breathing so heavily? Why does the air feel so oppressive? Why am I struck dumb, unable to move, unable to say anything? Why is my dog trembling, whimpering, and only next to me because I put his lead on and dragged the poor terrified creature upstairs to be near me when I knew the house didn't feel right; and could see a faint glow of light upstairs from his end of the landing, which shouldn't have been there? How do I know it could only be my brother?

I watch his door. I stare at it so hard it seems to get nearer to me and thus grow in size. All my senses must be acutely alert because I can smell my own fear and the fear in my dog. I can see tiny particles of dust in the air glinting in the faint evening light; and I can even

61

hear the blood coursing through my arteries and the loud constant regular thumping of my heart; fast, fast, fast. My mouth is so dry I can't even give a word of comfort to poor Thunder, even if I dared speak, which I daren't because I know it's him in there; and if he hears me he will speak to me, or worse, open the door and I don't know what I will see. And I can't run away because I can't move, and if I did see anything I might die of fright. And there is no-one to help because I am all alone apart from my one companion who has messed himself in his dreadful stress. And now I can see movement! Just shadows under the door of someone or something moving about in his room. Backwards and forwards, to and fro, and I want to scream and scream but I daren't, I really daren't. So I just stare transfixed and breathe so hard.

I start rocking myself and stroking the dog so severely it must be hurting him. I am resolved that I know it is only him in his room, and remind myself that he loved me. He told me so on the day he died. He came up to me; I was in the garden mowing the lawn and he had been playing with a friend of his. He approached me and signalled for me to stop the machine. 'I love you brother' he said and he hugged me. I was totally taken aback. We were close as brothers are, but he was five years younger than me and this was not the sort of behaviour we ever exhibited. A friendly punch perhaps and lots of wrestles and the like, but not a serious hug and such a message from an eleven year old; and he was only just eleven, his birthday had been the week before. I remember there was something very deep about his eyes that transfixed me and stopped me from replying. He smiled and walked away and I watched him depart wondering why he had come across so old and so much more mature than me. Within five minutes, his friend came to find me and tugged me towards the road. He said Timmy had been hit by a car and then started crying. It turned out that Timmy had been waiting to cross the road on the spot where I had been hit, but that some woman's car had mounted the pavement and taken his head off. She only stopped because she couldn't see through the windscreen for blood; I know that because once I had realised what had happened and seen his body, I ran after her car to stop her and she screamed abuse at me, and blamed me, and blamed Timmy, and blamed everyone but herself. That's why we never said he had an accident, we said he was killed; but she was just the instrument. He had known something was going to happen for weeks.

The nightmares started with the 'white lady' coming for him. At first we thought it was just like the nightmares I had had at his age called by my father, the 'screaming abdabs'. I would see cloudlike people in my room and hear voices. The worst nightmares were when I was in bed and would imagine crowds of people downstairs; then hear them all running upstairs together, and then my bedroom door would actually burst open, only for no-one to appear. His 'nightmares' were different however, because he was always awake, pointing above his head and shaking in terror. We of course tried everything apart from involving anyone outside the family. Mother used to sleep with him and that helped for a while, but it upset and annoyed my father. I slept in his room or sat with him, but I became scared myself when he would point to his white lady, pinch me tight and beg me to tell him why she was coming for him. We tried to pacify him with the thought that the white lady was Nana who before she had died had stayed with us, and would walk about at night in a white nightie and with her white hair making her look completely spectral. I remember sometimes his screaming was so scaring we would all of us huddle outside his room and stare at each other, lost in our own thoughts. None of us thought he was going to be killed. He never said he was going to die; but in those minutes before the very end, when he hugged me and told me he loved me, he knew without doubt he was no longer for this World. He was so calm and passive and just not Timothy, and it was in his eyes. And now he was in his room, and I could see him moving behind the door!

My parents were deeply into the supernatural. I don't mean they thought about ghosts or aliens or anything but they did wholeheartedly believe in fortune telling and the afterlife. From an early age I remember we always had babysitters who were called Aunties. None of them were actual aunties but it made them seem more child friendly I suppose. All of them were however, witches. Now I don't mean this from a perspective of their being anything other than kindly loving ladies, but they were all self-confessed witches and my parents revelled in it. Aunty May was the most fascinating and had the most influence on me. She must have babysat me from birth as I can remember her as a middle aged and then an old aged woman. Even before I could read she used to buy me a comic every week, sit me on her knee and read the words to me, and then when I had finally discovered the magic of reading for myself, I used to sit with her and painfully but exultingly take her through every caption of the Beano. She had a big thing about tea did Aunty May. She used to bring her own teapot with her and replenish it from a tall brown bottle kept hidden away in her large recessive handbag. She could get quite violent and throw things around, especially if Sammy the budgie was out of his cage. He would find a convenient perch and chant 'Aunty May's a bastard' over and over again. Sometimes she would throw beetroot for some reason, but this was always later in the evening around our bedtime when her teapot was empty and she wanted us out of the way so she could check the house was secure, especially the lounge where father had the spirits cabinet, and where anyone breaking in was bound to make for first of all, so she told us. (Many of Dickens' characters favour a teapot with their own special elixir within; most famous has to be the frightful nurse Mrs. Gamp in Martin Chuzzlewit. In fact I had a very Dickensian set of relatives when I was a very small boy. They lived in Leicester so would have been on my mother's side of the family. Uncle Percy had a very big nose, always wore a mustard coloured smoking jacket, spoke with a twist in his voice as if he had a stick of liquorice stuck in his throat and called me 'young sir'. He also took snuff regularly which made him sneeze profusely. His wife was called Aunt

Sissy; never moved from her chair where she actually had dust on her (although it could have been snuff from one of Uncle Percy's explosions) and would only drink from her own silver teapot, from which no-one else was allowed to partake, especially children. I remember trying to peep inside the spout once when she was napping and smelling something medicinal and getting a very watery eye.)

Aunty May would read Mum and Dad's teacups and so tell their fortunes, which always earned her an extra pound or two. Her big revelation was that if you had a large tealeaf left in your cup you were going to meet a dark stranger. The fact that this was the pre-teabag era; Mother only used to buy large leafed tea and so consequently we were forever about to be inundated with dark strangers; Aunty May may well have been as clairvoyant as Enoch Powell without the political bias. And yet she used to sit on my bed at night and talk about fairyland. She believed in elves, pixies, fairies, gnomes and the like and would try and make me do the same. I was especially scared of gnomes, so even though I was very very young when all this started, I tried my hardest to hide in my own safe World. This used to annoy Aunty May and she would bring her fairyland guide to sit on the bed with me to prove he was real. She would stand at the end of the bed and the bed would shake as he jumped up and down. I could feel the little feet hitting me through the blankets and eiderdown, and when he stopped, even see the impression of where he was sitting on the bed, but I never actually saw him and Aunty May was much displeased. She only babysat for Timmy for a few times because at the time we lived in Beckenham, and by now we had moved to the house built for Mother and Father, and that was too far away for May to come.

Enter Aunty Molly! She didn't need tealeaves or fairies, oh no, she was right out of the spirit-world. A strange woman, also keen on sherry (I was old enough to realise what was going on at this stage) and very hairy. She had very hairy legs, very hairy arms and a moustache which I could never understand why she didn't shave off. She also always wore the same brown dress and smelt less than fresh. Occasionally she would bring her mother with her who had the complete facial set and as my father used to say, would have been quite a draw in a travelling circus. All sins forgiven however because these two earned considerable sums by telling my parents lots of positive forecasts through spirit guides and the like which kept them happy.

The most disturbing soothsayer my parents had dealings with I never met, because he refused to meet me! His name was Travis; he was a dwarf and would tell my parents about their past lives. My father in particular was a very old soul, had existed in Arab lands long before the time of Jesus and was the deepest soul Travis had ever met. I have never traced my family tree but if I go back far enough on my father's side I am sure we are of very old Jewish extraction. Certainly my father believed this and some of the old fashioned photo's I still have of his parents and grandparents speak for themselves. Dad was a very kind loving man, jam-packed full of mischief, and you rarely saw him angry.

One relevant exception stands out however and that was just before Timmy died. The Tutankhamen exhibition was in London. There was of course a lot of hoo-hah about the curse of the Mummy and how Howard Carter and his associates had died mysterious deaths after discovering and breaking into the tomb. In fact in later years my mother met a very posh lady through the Brighton and Hove conservative association (who else), who had actually been at the opening of the tomb. The very elderly lady in question sadly died not long after she met my Mum thus fulfilling the prophesy in my Mum's eyes. The fact that they met this millennium and the tomb was found in 1922 never entered into it. Anyway, we were forbidden on pain of death to go and see the Tutankhamen relics, especially Timmy who was due to go and see this marvel on a forthcoming school trip. He duly went however, with my mother as an accomplice, and came home having drawn and coloured in a beautiful death mask of the boy King for my Mum. She said it was 'the best picture he had ever painted'. When my father learnt of this transgression he went ballistic, ranted and raved at my mother, tore the mask to shreds and took it outside and threw the pieces in the dustbin, probably one of the only real times I have ever seen him angry and to lose control.

It may sound as if I was sceptical about the spirit world, fairies, ghosts and the like. The fact is I am only too aware there is 'something else' but I know if I let myself succumb to the spine tingling sensations inside me every time something even remotely supernatural happens, it could very easily escalate out of control. I *had in my early teens played Ouija (forbidden in our house as whatever came in would never go away) with disturbing consequences; I had definitely seen together with three friends, a ghost in the local golf club snooker room; and had a number of very frightening spectral experiences, all of which I am sure a good therapist would put down to hormones and youth.*

My first real taste of another World from that we experience occurred in my early twenties. I had emigrated to South Africa at the age of twenty-one somehow having acquired a wife at that stage and we duly settled down to a very different way of life in Johannesburg.

The apartment block we ended up in was 1920's style architecture, with about a hundred nice sized apartments with art-deco interiors, and all clean and very well kept, mostly thanks to the servants. This was the Jewish sector of Jo'burg, the apartment having been let to me by one of my dad's friends called David, whose mother lived on the floor above us.

She was a charming, very graceful lady in her early eighties or so and we used to meet her often when we went to David's house for dinner. One evening I was having quite a deep conversation with her and she asked if I had ever been to a séance. I replied in the negative and said I didn't really believe in all the sitting round a table holding hands and hearing voices mumbo-jumbo I had seen in the movies. She laughed, and challenged me and my wife to watch a séance the following Sunday afternoon at her apartment.

When we subsequently nervously knocked at her door (I was scared I was going to laugh and embarrass myself), we were led through to her front facing and rather large lounge. Inside were seated seven or eight smiling and friendly looking ladies of similar age to our friend, seated in a loose circle with two spare seats in the circle obviously set aside for us. There was no table in the middle, the curtains were open and it was a lovely sunny tropical spring afternoon. I felt very relaxed and no longer worried about laughing as none of the staged environment I had imagined would set me sniggering was in evidence.

After some polite introductions, one particular elderly lady explained that the purpose of the meeting was to help spirits who did not know they were dead and thus needed to be shown the way to the light. She then asked us to hold hands and said a prayer to God to protect us from anything unwelcome coming through to us. She expressly said, looking at me, that the circle must not be broken whatever happens, as it could be dangerous. By now my mouth was dry, I felt intensely serious and very conscious of the fact I no longer wanted to be part of this, but that I had gone too far and had to see this through. After all, it was only a room full of old ladies, the blessed Sun was streaming in and there was no table through which to hear scary knocking. But I failed to console myself, I had had this feeling inside me before!

She asked us to put our hands on our laps, try and empty our minds of any conscious thoughts and sit still and quiet. I of course looked at everyone around the circle and glanced behind me to make sure we were alone in the room, but all was perfect calm.

Then it started to happen.

The air got very heavy and you could sort of hear a very faint buzzing sound emanating from the very people in the room, almost like the sound electricity makes through the wires at overhead pylons. Then very slowly and increasingly perceptibly, I could see one corner of the room behind the particular elderly lady begin to darken. Before long a shape made itself apparent and became the outline of a huge male figure. Before I could be alarmed the lady spoke to us in a soft and wonder filled voice.

'My spirit guide is with us', she said. 'He tells me he was a Medicine Man in an ancient native tribe from what is now America, and he is here to protect us and lead the lost souls to us for our help. Relax and let the energy flow through you.'

I stared hard at where the guide's outline was, trying to see a Red Indian figure but all I saw the harder I looked, was something incredible to see and so hard to describe. It was like seeing nothing, but everything, forever, all at once. If you can imagine having a 3D image of space, where you can see countless galaxies retreating, and expanding away from each other at a vast speed; but then the galaxies become pinpoints of light; and then even though you know they are still there, the vision becomes as black as velvet, but completely and utterly transparent; and at the same time so thick you imagine you could pick it up and hold it. That is what I saw, all within the shape of the Red Indian. And then I felt a strong tingling sensation at the base of my spine, and it felt as if something was inside my body squeezing my spinal cord, sending the sensation up towards my head; and I fought to stop that happening, and shouted 'no I don't want this', but not out loud; only in my head. And then I heard a little girl crying and calling for her Mummy, and saying she was lost, and why had she been left on her own. And then the ladies were talking sweetly to the voice, and telling her to look for a light and follow that light, and not to look anywhere else but at the light where people would be waiting for her. And then I noticed that the little girl's voice was coming from my wife and that she seemed to be asleep but that her eyes were open and only the whites were showing. And the voice was so totally alien to any sound my wife could make I knew it couldn't be hers.

I only went to the séance once again and that ended in disaster as stupidly I had agreed to take my boss along who had feigned interest but was really only there to mock and prove I had been duped. I have never before or since seen a wheelchair bound elderly lady stand up in a trance, angrily and very deliberately walk across the room, lift a fully grown man high above her head and smash him against the wall. I wouldn't have imagined that possible, but I could certainly believe a huge powerful Medicine Man could do that!

A crowd had gathered around Timmy when I got back from stopping the car that had hit him, the man from the Post Office opposite our house was acting as spokesman and wouldn't let me near my brother, but said to go and tell my Mum. He said the ambulance was coming and it would all be alright; I knew otherwise but felt a strange and massive sense of responsibility and so was sensible enough to play along. Mum was livid when I knocked on her bedroom door to tell her she must 'come at once'. She was due to go to the City to meet my dad and help entertain some important American clients at dinner followed by a West End show, and she was only half dressed and already running late. When she took sight of me however her attitude changed instantly, she went quiet and I gently tugged her downstairs and held her hand as I led her outside to where the ambulance people were waiting. For her sake, they pretended Timmy was still alive and had put an oxygen tent over his head to hide the reality as they took him and Mum to hospital. I went back to the house to telephone.

When I rang my father's office I was put through to his secretary Sheila who had worked for my dad for countless years and was like a part of the family. I could tell she had been crying when I was put through but that emotion instantly changed to one of delight and relief on hearing my voice.

'Your father is on his way home' she said 'He left just seconds ago. He had a premonition you had had

73

another accident and just left, he is in a terrible state, he will be so happy you are safe, I have been phoning you for ages.' But we must have been outside with Timmy. I put the phone down. There was no-one else to call; there were no mobiles in those days.

That evening, when reality had dawned, the three of us, Mum, Dad and I, sat in pitch darkness in the lounge of our house not speaking, but screaming a million thoughts at each other and into the ether albeit in total silence. We were numb.

All of a sudden the phone rang. The shrill sound shook us all but only my mother had the wherewithal to go through to the hall and answer it. My father and I could hear her gasp; it was Aunty May. Aunty May had felt something terrible had happened but didn't know what. We had not seen her for probably eight years and she was distraught and little comfort to Mum who could not, and would not explain, but just wanted to put the phone down and go back to her quiet but so noisy reverie. I don't remember going to sleep that night but I do remember the next morning answering the doorbell to find Aunty Molly standing outside on the step. She was very business-like and said 'I need to see your mother'; came in and went and sat with Mum in her room upstairs. She explained that Timmy had visited her in the night to say he was at a university, living with his Nana and very happy (Timmy was dyslexic which was little understood at the time and so had been sent to a special school where you didn't learn anything, you just drew and painted, made models, played with puppets and threw sand at the kids in wheelchairs. Consequently he hated school). He had also told Aunty Molly there was something next to his bed he wanted my Mum to have. Naturally on learning this we all went into his room to look, Molly included. We searched the bedclothes, looked under the bed, and went through his bedside cabinet but found nothing out of the ordinary, no message, no gift, no clue to anything. Mum, Dad and I were all three without saying anything, acutely aware of the strangeness of all that was happening around us.

Thunder and I are at the top of the stairs. All these strange events of a few months before had been rushing through my mind, so I knew it was Timmy. I daren't say anything to him in case he answers. Instead I talk to him in my head, over and over again. 'Timmy, is it you? Please don't speak but let me know it is only you. You need to go now brother as it is scaring me, I love you but it is scaring me.' I can cope with the thought of him answering through my head but not if I actually hear his voice because if that happens and I even see him walk towards me, everything I know and believe has gone and changed and the World is very different and I am only a kid. I can see the shadow movement in his room, but I don't want to run away because I don't think I would ever dare come back to the house and I don't feel physically threatened. It, is something else. So I go into my room with Thunder, close my door, lay on my bed hugging my dog close to me and listen. I listen so hard. I try to hear through the sounds that houses make but which you hardly ever notice, the central heating system, water flowing, creaking noises for no apparent reason. I was listening for his voice answering me in my head, but mostly I was listening for footsteps. I remembered the footsteps running up the stairs and the door bursting open; I remembered the footsteps in my nightmares; I remembered lying in the grass behind a low-lying wall and hearing a giant stamping along the road and seeing the shadow of his massive hands feeling in the bushes for children he could eat, and all my friends had escaped but I could not run fast enough, and he was getting ever nearer to me and unless I woke up and Mummy came in he would get me. I remembered Aunty May's garden full of fairyland creatures that looked up at you but never smiled. I remembered sheer terror in my worst nightmares. I remembered the people in the TV set that shouldn't be there, and pointing at them as I trembled and hugged my dad tight for protection.

I awoke with a start. My bedroom light was on as well as my sidelight - I didn't remember putting that on. I was still on my bed and fully dressed but Thunder was softly growling; not noisily but through his teeth like a sort of snarl I had never known him do before. You know when you have to do something but you don't want to do it, how leaden you can feel; utterly exhausted and decades older. It must be that feeling people get in the final minutes when they are led away to be executed, when they finally know this is it, there is no turning back, all the things they wanted to say or do but never took the time to say or do are now so much air. They hear those dreaded words, 'It is time!'. I knew I had to open my door and summon the courage to face whatever was outside on the landing. As I approached the door I could hear voices downstairs, not loud and not confrontational but it sounded like two men talking. I dreaded what I had to do but I opened the door just a peep and the voices got louder. The landing light was on; the stair light was on; and as far as I could tell, all the house lights were on, and the house was oppressively hot. With massive relief I realised that the voices were the radio playing in the lounge and not strangers or worse. But everything electrical in the house seemed to be on, the TV playing static, the washing machine, cooker, everything. By now I had crossed the point of no return and steadily made my way downstairs holding the stair-rail with a vice-like grip. I went into the living room and turned off the radio and TV and listened hard to the now silent house. But there were no people, no Timmy, no-one, nothing.

I sat with my back against the wall in the kitchen until morning arrived and with it the blessed daylight, then I went into the garage to turn off the mains electricity (there was no way I was going to turn things off room by room); and then I went down the road to see the mother of a friend of mine and told her my tale. She said Thunder and I could stay there until my parents got home and I could stay off school and help her around the house. She was a wonderful woman, very Yorkshire in her ways and very strict (she is the only lady who has ever actually hit me on the head with a rolling pin as women did in children's comics in the sixties; I got over it.) She did come to my house with me the next day, but neither of us wanted to go in, and we looked up at

Timmy's bedroom from the garden and couldn't see anything, so we stayed away until Mum and Dad got home a couple of days later. She kindly came with me to see my parents when their car pulled up on the drive and to back up my story. Of course everything seemed kind of silly and unreal once I saw Mum and Dad smiling and taking ownership of the house like nothing had happened. I even sort of convinced myself I might have imagined everything and it had been a dream, but Thunder knew. He knew Timmy had been in his room. They had to drag him into the house and he wouldn't go near the bottom of the stairs. He looked deep into my eyes as if to share a secret, and he and I both knew. His stress naturally rubbed off on me, so to console me, Mum did agree to finally put Timmy's toys in the loft; move his furniture around so it was less like a shrine; give the room a complete spring-clean, and so break the spell that had been there since that terrible time.

It was on the Sunday that Mum moved his room around; they had arrived home the previous Friday. Dad and I were sitting downstairs watching TV when Mum came slowly and deliberately into the room. She was white as a sheet, staring as if into nowhere, and clutching something tightly to her breast. She had moved his bedside cabinet and found a sheet of paper underneath. In trembling hands she held out to us the Tutankhamen death mask Timmy had drawn and coloured so lovingly for her. You could see the faint lines where it had been somehow pieced together, and it was 'the best picture he had ever painted'.

I knew he was in his room!

| TRAIN No.5 | CALLING AT: | *Matilda* |

It is a couple of weeks since I last caught this train to London, but sitting in the same part of the carriage, albeit on the opposite side of the aisle facing me is – the Unlikely Gentleman. Nothing much has changed about him. He stills looks filthy, squalid, unwashed and unshaven; but this time he has a particularly strange looking friend sitting next to him. I can tell he is a friend, because he has just passed a small plastic bag of something that looks suspiciously like green stringy tobacco across, which the Unlikely Gentleman has swiftly jammed into his trouser pocket, and which has made him look even more furtive. Perhaps it is simply his birthday.

Attempting to ignore their increasingly loud and obnoxious conversation, I am today trying to study some biology and the origins of life.

I learn that no matter how we end up, every one of us starts life as a single cell called a zygote, but that we swiftly multiply into an organism consisting of countless trillions of cells that fall into a couple of hundred or so categories. The Unlikely Gentleman's friend looks so much like a misshaped blob, and is so lacking in definition with few if any distinguishing features, perhaps he is simply a zygote that grew enormous without ever dividing itself and diversifying.

My book also tells me that our body replaces old cells with new ones at a rate of millions per second, and that apart from very specialist cells, most cells in the body have been completely replaced after seven years. This means that if you look at yourself now, everything you can see of yourself which is living (i.e. not nails and hair), is no more than seven years old; we regenerate *Doctor Who* style. Unfortunately stem cells and brain cells don't regenerate which is why we get old and die, and as most people know we lose brain cells at a swift pace, although fortunately we start with billions and billions. Most people also know that alcohol and drugs are a good way of killing off these spoil-sport brain cells, and I can tell from the waft of stale drink permeating from across the carriage, and the huge dilated pupils of the giant zygote, that he has become a dab hand at trying to get rid of as many as he can, in as short a space of time as possible.

As I contemplate this odd couple out the corner of my eye however, my nose does sense mixed in with the drink smell and rank body odour, a somewhat sweeter and more herbal aroma, possibly emanating from the packet I saw pass hands. My own brain cells swiftly react to this stimulus, unwittingly recalling memories of much younger days…

MATILDA

The last time I smoked marihuana was at Monkey Bay in Malawi, a country correctly marketed as 'the warm heart of Africa'; and that was in the early eighties, some thirty years ago. My first time was also in Africa albeit a couple of years earlier.

As a teenager I don't remember drugs being a big thing. I never came across drugs at school, and even though this was just after the swinging sixties, the whole drug scene seemed to be more for rock stars, fashion models and the film set. I did however have some friends in the next village to me who lived in posh houses and went to a posh school, and they and I would occasionally meet up at weekends and usually end up in someone's bedroom late in the evening listening to music. There, the others would pass around a joint made up of tobacco with scrapings of hashish thrown in for good measure. Where this hashish had come from was always surrounded with an air of mystery by the person who had obtained it. Some would claim to have paid a huge sum for their small chunk of brown goo; others would have got it cheap because they were 'in with the supplier', the latter of whom was always a decidedly dastardly character, probably wearing a trench coat, a battered homburg, a shifty look, and whose eyes were far too close together. I tried this substance of wonder once, desperately trying to feel some effect but to no avail, so instead I would bring along to our soirées a bottle of wine for myself. After a few puffs, my friends would change country of origin using words such as cool; hay; man; hay man; cool man; hay cool man; and other possible permutations, and nodding a lot as they sat crossed legged listening to heavy rock and playing air guitar. I also felt cool because I was drinking either Blue Nun or Black Tower liebfraumilch which although I hated the sweet taste, was cheap and either had a 'cool' label (Blue Nun) or was in a 'cool' bottle (Black Tower). So I would also nod, say 'man' a lot, not to feel too out of place, and we would all end up neither stoned nor drunk because I am sure the hashish was always fake, and they used to pinch most of my wine.

I had been living in South Africa for two years by now and had somehow managed to divorce my wife and mistakenly managed to acquire a new fiancée. It seemed like prime time to quickly evaporate elsewhere, and quite by chance a Rhodesian friend called Chris and I had been talking about travelling across the continent from Cape to Cairo, the great dream. Within a few short weeks we had both given up our jobs; bought and made ready a wonderful old Land Rover that had already seen a lot of Africa (for serious buffs: it was a series three, long wheel base, petrol version, beige bottom and white top, full length roof rack and with two spare tyres, one of course situated on the bonnet); and spent lots of the bank's money on provisions, necessities and things we didn't need at all but decided to take with us just for the sake of it and because we had the space. In those days banks didn't give you a bank guarantee card, so if you paid for items by cheque, the retailer having deemed you to look bona-fide, the bank picked up the tab if the cheque subsequently bounced. This only worked however if you were intent on fleeing the country before the bank cottoned on to you. We duly said goodbye to fiancée and friends and fled. The fact that we did not depart from the Cape, Johannesburg being 1000 kilometres further north, and the fact that we never got to Cairo doesn't matter one jot; we had a fantastic time and the experience of a lifetime.

Our first serious setback on this year of adventure didn't occur until at least five hours into our journey, by which time we had crossed the magically named Limpopo River, left South Africa and were in no man's land at the border crossing with Botswana. It was only at this stage when handing over all our papers that we realised the Land Rover was still in the name of the guy we had bought it from. In our excitement of planning our trip this was something we had simply and stupidly overlooked. I remember the black Botswanan border official looked **very** official and **very** smart in a nice new uniform, so we knew we had a real problem on our hands. It is at times like this that I have always found that if you are smartly dressed, hold yourself well, look the part (whatever that part is supposed to be), and are extremely polite and conciliatory you can get away with almost anything. Acting as if we were letting him in on some massive secret, (looking over our shoulders and talking in a sideways manner), we told the very official official what a hurry we had been in to leave South Africa because some angry women were after us; how the vehicle had been a gift from an old man who understood our plight and other such complete rubbish; all of the time looking more and more forlorn, until to our delight, he proudly sat erect on his stool and winking at us with a knowing leer on his face, stamped our passports and waved us into his country! One day I will go and properly explore Botswana as it is a beautiful country. At the time we were there however, there was a major conflict going on in its near neighbour Angola across the Caprivi Strip which was spilling disastrously into Botswana. On entering 'black' Africa we also suddenly felt very exposed. We had left South Africa in a hurry; we were in a vehicle not registered to us; we were surrounded by war zones; and we were driving a vehicle we had filled with so much desirable equipment, medicines, cigarettes and hidden American dollars, we were literally sitting inside a gold-mine on wheels. So we made as fast as possible for the town of Plumtree, and the relative safety of the border 500 kilometres north with Zimbabwe-Rhodesia, as that country had just been renamed.

The saying was that when you entered Rhodesia you had to set your watch back twenty-five years, and they were right. The country had been suffering sanctions from most of the rest of the World for wanting independence from Britain. At the same time Rhodesia was literally just ending a civil 'communist fed' bush war in which eventually (a few years after I had left), and with Britain's collusion, everyone's favourite at the time Uncle Bob Mugabe would come out tops – what a success story that has been!

We knew our Land Rover was old, but as soon as we entered the country I was taken back to my childhood by seeing what would have been dream cars when I was five years old, still in pristine condition and being driven sedately along smart but relatively empty roads as petrol was in very short supply. Very soon we were in the southern capital of Matabeleland, Bulawayo, famous for its wide streets laid out by its founders so that a complete span of oxen could turn a cart round without having to reverse. Chris was from that town and so having met a few old acquaintances we did the grand tour ending up at the railway station. Here I was rewarded with the amazing sight of at least twenty mighty steam engines being fired up to pull the immense coal trains down to South Africa, the one country still buying goods from Rhodesia. I have always been a steam buff, but the sight at dusk of so many huge black engines bellowing steam and smoke, with their cabs lit up as if each had created its own mini sunset (coupled with the incredible smells and sounds) was truly awe-inspiring.

That night we stayed with some friends of Chris', a wonderful Italian family, and I learnt how hard things had been even for the relatively wealthy. It was a large family as most Italian families are with granny, mum, dad, five children and two aunties. Together with Chris and I this made for quite a table and we all sat down expectantly. The menu that night was spaghetti Bolognese, as it was apparently most nights. Now, I hate pasta, but as guest of honour I was presented with an enormous bowl of pure white wriggling worms topped with the only, and I mean only spoonful of Bolognese sauce, everyone else just having worms. I was watched jealously by the other diners as I gulped the sauce and then with increasing malevolence as they realised I was going to leave most of the worm-food having stolen their dream topping. We left early the next day!

Our next stop was the magnificent, but sadly lacking in live animals game reserve with the school-boyishly amusing name of Wankie. This was once a magnificent game park and hopefully will be once again, but at the time, most of the warring factions had been using the dense forests in the park as a base, and had either killed the animals for food, left enough land mines to do the job for them, or made the surviving animals so violent towards man that visitors were even rarer than some of the most protected species. It was also hard to get permission to enter because of all the above.

By this time we had attired ourselves in our best 'we have been travelling through Africa for years' clothes. These consisted of obligatory tan coloured shorts with lots of pockets, a heavily starched green shirt with lots of pockets, long green socks over which we wore tough-looking bush shoes (but without the secret compass or magnet in the heel as they didn't do adult sizes), a neckerchief (bandana) because that's what they wear in cowboy films, a belt with more pockets for some reason or other, and a bush hat. My hat had a band round it which I was assured by the smiling South African salesman, would be replaced by an exotic snakeskin as soon as I killed my first exotic snake, assuming it didn't have similar aspirations towards me. I had also grown a pathetic attempt at a beard which I was inordinately proud of, used to pull tufts of and play with constantly as if that would make it grow even faster, and which produced a loud cheer from those I knew when many months later it was eventually cast down the plughole never to return (and yes the water does go the other way round the hole in the southern hemisphere).

We pulled up at the Ranger Headquarters of Wankie and strolled in nonchalantly, in our 'David

Attenboroughish' attire, to pay our entry fee and organise our stay, as you do.

'You guys must be from Chobe!' said the young 'Attenboroughish' styled man behind the desk, holding himself in a fawning way.

'Come again?' exclaimed we.

'I can see your badge on your Land Rover - wait until the boss knows you're here - you will be special guests - forget paying – wow we don't get many visitors like you here – what's it like in Chobe with the war and all, oh wow!, Oh wow!'

What we were thrilled to realise: We had named our Land Rover Chobe, meaning elephant in African, and had painted the name together with a picture of an elephant on each of the side doors, solely because it looked cool – very cool. Therefore, the rangers at Wankie obviously thought we were from Chobe game reserve in Botswana. Not only could we obtain permission to pass through the park, we could get in for free and be respected as fellow rangers. We duly signed in.

What we were not thrilled to realise: The head ranger at Wankie knew the head ranger at Chobe very well and was delighted to meet us; but then started asking awkward questions about his friend's health and welfare, the number of animals in the park, the status of the elephant herds in particular; and seemed a little perturbed by our confused answers, although we did a sterling job of telling lies, smiling a lot, looking very much the part, then saying how tired we were because of all the animals we had been counting and so forth, and wouldn't it be a good idea if we went and had a lie down.

'I will see you again at breakfast' said the now scary head ranger, 'In the meantime park and camp where you like, I am sure you know what you are doing!'

Not wanting to be questioned any further we duly drove to what looked like a pleasant area sufficiently far enough outside the walled compound where normal visitors would stay, and set up camp. It was late afternoon by this time but the weather was warm with beautiful blue skies, we were surrounded by acacia trees and low scrub thorn, and it having just been the wet season the grass beneath our feet was thick and lush. We collected some wood from beneath the trees for an evening fire – ever cautious of snakes despite my hat being in want of one; put up our tent, proudly set up the canopy shelter that fitted onto our Land Rover, established our two stripy deckchairs and sat with beer in hand taking in the majestic sounds, scents and vista of real true native Africa.

As dusk approached and the horizon became a mix of deep purple and azure, a man appeared. Now this seemed to happen a lot in Africa. Whenever we would stop and pull off the road, and in no matter how remote a region, a man would appear.

This man was obviously a local tribesman (a famous Matabele warrior as he later told us! In fact most 'men who appeared' seemed to be ex-famous warriors from one tribe or another); he was about forty years of age, wearing a very old and moth-eaten suit, and also wearing a massive smile from ear to ear.

'I am your man!' he declared clapping his hands together a few times. 'I will make fire, I will cook, I will make tea, I will clean up, I will make sure no snakes come into camp'. All this of course sounded delightful, so we sat back, let him get on with things and thoroughly enjoyed hearing him chat away about life and times in Rhodesia.

After a while Chris put on some music. Before leaving Johannesburg we had installed a decent cassette player in Chobe, linked to two huge speakers by the back door, and nailed up a shelf above the driver's compartment full of a mixture of Chris' and my music. We had everything from classical to Abba, heavy metal to Ub40, and rock to Barbara Streisand. By now the light had virtually gone, the fire was burning just enough to be kept going with the addition of an occasional small log, we had eaten, and the three of us sat amicably and peaceably round the fire.

'Can you lay your hands on some special smokes?' says Chris to our new friend, who duly disappears beyond the firelight and within minutes reappears within the firelight, with an even bigger smile than usual and a large packet of 'mbanje'. For this and his services we exchange a bar of soap (African soap is about three times the length of our soap bars), some soup tins and a snazzy (read horrible) seventies style black nylon satin shirt from my collection, which he ensures us will win him any woman he wants at the local African disco, and off he goes to find out.

I stir up the fire because by now we can see many distant pairs of eyes looking at us with interest through the darkness, and because that internal human spirit tells us that a fire will keep us safe. Chris creates what will be my first real 'joint', and we settle back in our chairs to watch the tea brew on the fire in our wonderful, immense, beige coloured, Polish enamelware teapot that went everywhere with us – and ended up black, extremely battered, but much loved.

Imagine a balmy evening, the earthy almost ethereal smell of Africa, faint but not threatening animal sounds from afar; the added smell of a log fire and its accompanying crackling sounds as a log breaks in two; the crimson glow from a wood fire with yellow and blue darts piercing through as a slight breeze disturbs its peace and sends small red stars upwards into the black night; the sight of an ever growing heaven of real stars and dust patch galaxies above you; the knowledge that you are on the precipice of what could be a forever adventure; and the feeling that Africa is holding you in it's very embrace - loving you for being you, reminding you that this is where we came from as a species, so very long ago. This is how I felt, totally at peace, and brimming with the fullness of life.

Chris handed me a joint, I inhaled deeply, and 'brimmed' even more. There was no tobacco in this joint; this was pure 'grass'. It made my cheeks ache inside and tasted uniquely herbal. I also felt my smile increase to such a proportion I was sure if anyone could have seen me they would have thought me a clown. We sat and relaxed and smoked and sat and relaxed and smoked and I must have dozed or gone into a trance.

All of sudden I could hear animals, really loudly and really close. It sounded like hyenas or jackals or something even worse, and I tried to alert Chris.

'You bloody idiot' he laughed, 'I have put on *Animals* by Pink Floyd, the sounds are on the tape!' How we laughed and laughed, because this was perhaps the funniest thing ever, and we were in the middle of nowhere and so it became funnier still. We carried on listening and chuckling, and then I thought I saw what looked like a rhino's head in the shadow cast by the fire between Chobe and the nearest bush beyond. 'Look' said I, 'now I can **see** animals. Perhaps I'm like that arsehole Doctor Doolittle and can talk to them as well!'

The mirth increased as the evening unfolded. I made copious amounts of tea as for some reason we were evermore thirsty the more we smoked. The tea itself was wonderful locally grown tea mixed with sugar and tinned Carnation milk as fresh milk was unavailable. The more we smoked the more we drank and the more we smiled. After a while Chris thought he saw a rhino as well. It was behind me and nodding thoughtfully he surmised. We giggled like little girls.

By now I was at the surreal stage where I was able to take a back seat and watch what I was doing from afar, as if I was floating above our camp. I could see myself attempting to make tea and see me making a mess of things and almost fall into the fire, I could see Chris rock with laughter in his deckchair for no apparent reason and then nearly fall out of his chair, I could tell the music had stopped but had lost all knowledge as to how to remedy the situation, and I could hear myself talking to a large spectral rhinoceros standing between Chris and I, and improbably looking at the fire which glimmered in its half closed eyes. I only remember its head - all huge and knowing.

Somehow we must have got to bed because we awoke with the loudest dawn chorus known to man, but magically we were inside our tent and in our sleeping bags.

Strangely and incredibly ravenously hungry, we made our way into the compound and via the washrooms to the small but quaint thatched restaurant for breakfast. There we were met by an attractive but 'Attenboroughish' young lady member of the ranger team.

'I understand you stayed outside in the park last night, she said, 'that was brave of you.'

'Well we're from Chobe' said I in a massively bighead voice and trying to show I had a beard by thrusting my chin out, and holding my precious bush hat in such a way that she could obviously see it, 'we know what we are doing!'

'I see you met Matilda!' said a voice not dissimilar to the dreaded head ranger's and coming from behind me.

'Matilda?' said I turning round to face said head ranger and assuming he meant the young 'Attenboroughish' girl.

'Yes. I should have warned you but you seemed so confident. Matilda is the rogue rhino who has been bothering the camp and is known to be very violent. I watched you through my field glasses last night. I was going to come out with a gun to scare her off but you were so calm with her, you really **do** know your stuff'.

Arrggghhhhhhhhhhh!!!

The next few months took us through many books'-worth of stories; to the majestic Victoria Falls and its unique rainforest; through Zambia and the Copperbelt; down the Zambezi River and some of its hippo infested tributaries; back into Zimbabwe at Lake Kariba where we fished for 'tigers' in the ghost-ridden sunken forest of Matusadona; finally leaving that country from the capital Salisbury (now Harare) to travel to Malawi across Mozambique. That final part was the nearest we came to being killed. We were perhaps the only white civilians to have crossed Mozambique through the route we took for a number of years. The country was in the grip of civil war between communist backed troops and their South African backed opponents. We were in communist held territory and driving a vehicle with the registration letters TJ (Transvaal, Johannesburg), so unmistakably of South African origin. There were four things that kept us alive. Firstly, at every checkpoint where machine guns were pointed at our heads by young, sometimes child soldiers, and we were quizzed in broken Portuguese – not a word of which we understood; we had an endless supply of American cigarettes to buy our way forward. Secondly we were very friendly, conciliatory, polite, and wore huge smiles. Thirdly, purely by chance we had a POLICE sticker on the windscreen from the latest *Police* album, and that lent us an air of authority. And fourthly, when I was caught by some very angry soldiers, photographing an enormous tank base of Russian T52 tanks in the town of Tete, and Chris and I were held on the dusty ground with rifles pressing into our temples ready to blow our heads off, I remembered what one traveller we had met had said if we ever got into such a scrape – 'use the words BBC'. So I did, over and over, 'BBC', 'BBC', 'BBC', and sure enough after a few moments of confusion, shouting, and being buffeted, an officer appeared who spoke some English, took some money and cigarettes off us, smashed my camera, and told us to get out of his country by nightfall or we would be shot. Thank-you BBC – I really mean that.

That night we sat in the Land Rover on the wrong side of the Mozambique/Malawi border, as the gates had already closed by the time we arrived there. The rain was torrential, we were starving, and there was nothing to eat at the local shop. Literally all they had to sell were some seeds, a barrel of old Coca-Cola style drink and some green tomatoes, all of which we bought anyway and mixed to make a disgusting soup which we shared with some African lorry drivers. We were also fearfully expecting at any moment to see soldiers arrive to make sure we had left the country, but mercifully we were left alone.

Morning arrived and there was an inevitable dispute over our papers. We were told we would have to go back to Tete, a fate that filled us both with dread. Finally however, it emerged that the road ahead had been washed away it being the rainy season, and a senior official needed to get to Blantyre in Malawi as soon as possible. The only vehicles available were lorries, and these were stuck fast in the mud with no chance of negotiating the steep terrain on dirt roads even if they had been able to move. Would we take him in our Land Rover if they let us through – er, yes we would!

And so on the 30th April 1981 and breathing massive sighs of relief we drove safely into the wonderful country of Malawi, the warm heart of Africa, and it was my twenty-fourth birthday!

```
┌─────────────────────────────────────────────┐
│                                             │
│  TRAIN No.6   CALLING   The Lucky Beans      │
│               AT:                            │
│                                             │
└─────────────────────────────────────────────┘
```

I only just caught the train this morning which is thankfully quiet, it being the summer holiday period. I am perusing an Astronomy journal and an article in which it is interesting to see how telescope names have changed over the years. From being named after famous astronomers of the past such as Hubble, Herschel et al, we evolve to more recent naming conventions such as the 'Large Telescope' in Southern Africa which is big; the 'Very Large Telescope' in Chile which is bigger; the 'Extremely Large Telescope' run by the European Space Observatory which is huge; and the planned 'Overwhelmingly Large Telescope' also planned by Europe, and which will be the biggest of them all.

I can see approaching my table an 'overwhelmingly large lady' and an 'extremely large boy'. Of course, they choose to sit at my table despite all the others being completely vacant, otherwise how could they hope to ruin my astronomical musings.

In a more gentle age when such vast expanses of living flesh were perhaps rarer, these two might well have been described as Jolly. In fact in old texts we read many instances of Jolly Friars, the Jolly Pie-man and his Jolly wife, the Jolly Farmer and such-like. In all such cases we are able to envisage the character in question without any visual aid, any woodcut or illustration of the characters in question, merely serving to enable us to nod and smile with satisfaction at our correct prior mental depiction.

As time moved on, authors in the early Victorian era tended to be more circumspect of their description of large people. I cite by way of example my favourite writer William Harrison Ainsworth (the gentleman who wrote about and glorified the genuine highwayman Dick Turpin, and who invented his horse Black Bess), who describes a baker's wife thus:- 'she was of middling height and bright of eye, with an interesting turn of ankle, but she tended to exceed the rules of symmetry!' Later in the same century Charles Dickens takes on the mantle but doesn't hold back. In describing the female owner of a way-side inn he states that she is 'a big, fat, heavy-faced personage'. No supporting picture needed *there* Charles.

Now, in the twenty-first century, I have to think of these two fellow travellers as being clinically obese, but that it is unlikely to be their own fault, it all being the responsibility of their genes; clever little chunks of our DNA that help make us what we are. Sure enough however (and as I had secretly suspected), no more than two minutes into their journey, the mother (I have ascertained this from the boy's piglet-like squeal 'you're squashing me Mum, you fat cow!') opens her copious hold-all and starts to provide her own and her offspring's genes with a steady supply of sugar rich consumables, especially noisy crisps; potted something or other of a very smelly persuasion; oh, and some packets of dried fruit and beans, which at least are good for you, unless laced with salt as theirs clearly are, as disclosed by the crystals the woman is busy licking off her grotesquely swollen fingers. The extremely large boy also manages to make a disgusting sound as he suckles lustily from a fizzy pop bottle. Perhaps he is a budding Benny Goodman but Mother can't afford a real Clarinet.

As I am forced to watch this gluttony and place my article to one side – I think on about what the boy called his substantial parent. I must say I consider him calling his mother fat albeit honest, was somewhat brusque, but in his defence felt sure that rather than his use of the word 'cow' suggesting she was also of the bovine persuasion, he was perhaps making use of an abbreviation previously unknown to me, C.O.W., 'Clinically Obese Woman'.

Isn't there a famous children's story about a boy, a cow, and some beans?..

THE LUCKY BEANS

After months of living in countries suffering from sanctions, civil wars or pure financial mismanagement, we had arrived in what appeared to be at the time a small haven in the middle of all this chaos. Malawi is a relatively small African country set in the tropical southern hemisphere and bordered by Mozambique, Zambia, Zimbabwe and Tanzania. Being relatively stable unlike its neighbours, stopping refugees flooding the country and crippling the economy was a major problem even back in the 1980's. President Banda was in charge of things and if memory serves me well, famous for having been found under a magical tree somewhere in the forest and thus destined to lead his nation; and not as some evil minded wags claimed, that he arrived by plane from Britain where he had been a practising Doctor and had ditched his white girlfriend and mother of his only child. Anyway, none of that was my concern. We pulled into the Malawi Sun hotel in Blantyre, had much needed showers and a change of clothes and went expectantly into lunch. To my delight we could order (and get served with) wine, really nice ice-cold beer, cheddar cheese, milk, fruit and the best fish I have ever tasted, a white fish called Chambo from lake Malawi. The lake by the way is 365 miles long by 52 miles wide, easy to remember as the days and weeks of the year. Unfortunately it does get wider every year to the detriment of lakeside hotels as Mozambique built a dam to create their own lake, and this has backed up the Zambezi river all the way to its source - a typical case of sod the people upstream. Lunch lasted at least four hours, an amazing feat at the time (only to become standard practice when I worked in the City of London many years later). We also met a family of local mixed race lads who invited us to stay on their farm with them if we could give them a lift home as the roads had been flooded and were no longer existent…..so we did.

Much adventure later we were heading north and found ourselves out of petrol on the road from Blantyre to Zomba, the old capital of the country and seat of the President's palace.

We quickly learnt that no fuel was expected in the country for at least two weeks as all the foreign currency reserves had run out, a regular occurrence in that part of the World. So out came the stripy deckchairs, the trusty teapot and utensils, and as can be expected, a man arrived and made a fire for us.

Can we get some mbanje? asks Chris as usual. Our man laughs and waves his arms around his head.

"No, mbanje, you know, special smoke!" says Chris misunderstanding the man's gesture.

Our man takes Chris by the hand and leads him to the field behind us, where to his amazement he is presented with literally acres and acres of the best 'mbanje' in Africa, Malawi Gold. You could just walk into a field and pick a huge cob, as big as a sweet-corn and it was all free. The silly thing was however, if you were caught with any, it was the death sentence. They also hanged you for rape in Malawi (not that we were contemplating any - and by the way the hangman was British, and visited Malawi every so often especially to carry out his trade), but they only gave you a few years' hard labour for murder.

Sitting by the road for two days and watching life go by, with no traffic except that on two legs or the occasional bullock or bus, we quickly realised that the whole country must be stoned. Nobody seemed to walk in a straight line, going from side to side of the road and always in a laughing, smiling, happy, completely unhurried way. Even the buses were completely unhurried and always had a laughing, smiling, happy driver, and travelled sideways. This was because all the roads were single track so if a bus met another vehicle coming towards it, it would have to go half off the road and into the rutted mud, thus damaging the suspension on the left hand side, and after a few months of this, a crab-like movement would become the norm. This never mattered until the now designated crab-bus met an oncoming vehicle, in which case everything else had to career off the road into the trees and scrub, risking wiping out cattle, dogs, cyclists, and even houses just to avoid being swept into oblivion by this bus menace - great fun to watch however. We also learnt some of the local language from the Chichewa people who would all stop and chat with us as they passed by, and learned that basically every male calls every other male 'Bambo', unless he is deemed to be mad, like us, in which case he is called what sounded like 'Jimmy Sorrow'.

After a few days of this forced entertainment, an old battered and weather-beaten truck pulled to a halt in front of us and out stepped an old battered and weather-beaten farmer, also called Jimmy. He seemed to know everyone in Malawi and so couldn't understand where we two stupid looking individuals fitted in. It didn't help that by now my beard had grown to the extent that if you had turned my head upside down, you would not have been able to tell the difference, and the fact that Chris had attempted to grow a Cary Grant moustache. When he learned that we had come through the Mozambique war-zone however, he wanted to hear more, and let us siphon off enough fuel from the truck to follow him to his home.

Home was on a beautiful tobacco estate of many hundreds of acres, employing a few hundred well looked after workers who lived there with their families. Jimmy's homestead was in the middle of the estate and was like a large English bungalow but surrounded by exotic tropical plants and fruit trees galore. We were all welcomed by Jimmy's lovely wife Shirley, the ultra efficient housekeeper Samson, and the bull terriers, Bella and Mr. Smith. We soon learned over lunch that Bella was Mr. Smith's mum, and that she was placid and Mr. Smith was anything but. He was completely white and named after Ian Smith, the ex-premier of Rhodesia in whose regime Jimmy had been a high ranking official. Mr. Smith's three favourite pastimes were chasing the workers on the estate, sitting on anyone whenever possible, and killing and ripping to shreds the vervet monkeys that would tease him remorselessly. If the front door was closed, they would even throw fruit through the house window at him and then laugh and show their bottoms at him whilst he went berserk with indignation, and was inconsolable until let out to try for his revenge.

We very quickly fitted in as if we were two long lost sons, especially with Shirley, which was just as well because after three days, Jimmy broke a leg and we had to take on running the estate. In typical fashion we had been sitting on the stoop late evening, Jimmy, Chris and I, listening to the insects, the distant drumming and happy sounds from the village on the estate, staring at the then unknown to me constellations, and listening to Jimmy's wonderful stories of the old Rhodesia. Perched between us we had a case of Malawi Carlsberg beer and would take it in turns to walk into the darkness and have a pee on the lawn every few bottles or so. Jimmy was adamant that no water should ever be wasted in such a country and so the inside toilet was out of bounds to all males. On what must have been Jimmy's fifth turn there was a loud crash and we ran to find him lying on his back and wriggling like a pinned beetle, all except one leg that looked a bit out of shape.

For the next few weeks we ran the estate for him. This was most onerous and consisted of being driven around the estate twice a day by the foreman, and waving majestically in 'Queen Elizabeth fashion' from the vehicle to show that there was actually someone in charge. Once a week I also had the grand title of 'Paymaster General' which duties involved sitting for an entire morning in a hut paying the workers the amounts told to me by the foreman, thanking them for their hard work and commitment, and then spending the afternoon in the same hut changing the money I had paid them into smaller denominations because I had completely messed up the first time around, and the foreman was too polite to tell me. In my English view of the world, if I had earned twenty pounds, a nice new twenty pound note would be the thing to have. In the African view of things, a nice new twenty pound note can a; easily get lost so saying goodbye to a week's wages b; easily be stolen by a nasty big threatening man with a nasty big threatening stick who would like a nice new twenty pound note for himself; and c; be completely useless as legal tender as no-one for hundreds of miles around is going to be able to change it. 'Paymaster General' does look dashingly good on the 'job experience' part of my CV however, although this and other sort of glib comments (e.g. Ranger, Hotelier, Master Electrician) did stop me getting a job as a milkman upon my return to the UK. This was on the basis that the boss of the dairy felt,

'This CV is bloody unlikely young man, and only goes to reinforce my first instinct that for the past year (where you can't prove where you've been), you have either been in jail or on the run. Trust you with money and a milk-float? Not bloody likely!'

An opportunity sadly lost. Thank God for the London insurance industry where the similar reaction at first interview was,

'This is bloody unlikely young man. Trust you with thousands of pounds of our customers' money? Can you hold your drink? You can - come and see where you will be sitting!'

The story of our having arrived via Mozambique spread quickly and we were soon invited to a curry lunch at the Zomba Gymkhana Club by the General of the Malawi army. This was a great honour and we made many friends with the officer corps, all of whom were black and all of whom loved the British, having been trained at Britain's expense at Sandhurst. With fuel for our own vehicle still being in short supply, we were now picked up most days by the military, chucked into the

107

back of an army truck, driven all over the country, and shown a fantastic time. I even remember meeting the sole honorary white Malawian, a very eccentric Scotsman living in a bungalow on the hill opposite Zomba Palace. If ever an Englishman's idea of a typical Scot existed, this was he. Medium height fat man but broad and strong, almost violent looking and with a massively vicelike grip; big white beard with yellow ochre coloured streaks giving away his original ginger heritage; mad twinkling blue eyes turned a pale azure from the Sun, set in a ruddy brown rugged face with more lines than Doctor Beeching closed; a strange mustard coloured large pocketed topcoat reminiscent of the late nineteenth century complete with weskit and tartan trews; an all pervading odour of Clan pipe tobacco from every crevice, pore and stitch; and when he violently shouted his unintelligible words of greeting, an overpowering waft and fine mist of warm whiskey and stale beer. His entire house was covered floor to ceiling in tartan to an extent that if he stood still he appeared legless, seemingly floating on a miasma concocted of drink and smoke. But he had taught the Malawi army officer corps to sword-dance – with real swords, and dance they did, to our utter amazement, everyone's delight, until it was time to be collectively thrown into the back of the lorry and driven merrily home, singing Scottish ballads no-one knew the correct words to.

Another memorable adventure with our army officers occurred whilst we were being driven in an army convoy up to Lake Malawi for some 'fun'. Chris and I were in a vehicle with four others and we had stopped for a roadside pee. I had been sat on my own scrunched in the back of the vehicle and was bored with the view having made the journey a few times previously, and also a little travel sick only having a side-on perspective. Before we re-embarked I noticed some really huge interesting looking bean pods on a plant at the edge of a field by the roadside, which I picked with a view to opening and exploring these on the next part of the journey. Sure enough as we were once again jolting along I cracked open a pod and discovered the most massive beans; they were smooth and oval in shape, a dark dusky pink in colour and wearing black shiny hats. More fascinating however was the thick fur on the pod itself which came off easily when plucked and could be blown into a puff of fine hairs which looked and danced like tiny airborne ballerinas – very sweet to see, very mesmerising and so addictive to view I quickly managed to spread as many of these swirls of choreographed beauty as I could throughout every crevice of the vehicle.

After a short while I began to feel itchy – very itchy. I could feel things crawling under the skin of my hands and lower arms. I naturally started scratching which naturally made things worse. Next to feel this attack was my neck and shoulders, the itching spreading as a shiver does in the depths of winter, right down to my tail at the bottom of my spine. I started to shout to the others something was wrong and then my eyes starting burning. I of course rubbed them, and the burning instantly changed to hot pokers being thrust into the sockets. I was yelling and could hear others in similar distress and through my streaming tears discerned the rest of the vehicle in total chaos as everyone jigged from side to side, up and down and beat themselves into a frenzy to escape the itching nightmare. I gauged the more I cried out the less I would itch and all the others seemed to have the same idea - the cacophony was deafening. Eventually the driver could take no more and crashed into a ditch and we all ran away from the broken vehicle screaming, leaping maniacally and hitting each other in a vain attempt to alleviate each other's suffering. Finally we all stripped off our clothes and used all our stock of precious water to assuage the nightmare that was attacking us. Naked, red eyed and still wriggling by the road-side, and being observed with much mirth by a local populace (some of whom were in that universal pose of bending forward holding their knees, leaning back to laugh at the sky, tipping earthwards again, and then starting the process all over as if they were those glass-blown perpetual motion machines). The officers, Chris and I looked at one another, then collectively and questioningly at me. I reluctantly opened my hand and held out my beans with a simpleton 'Look Mother, I swapped these for our cow' expression and awaited the inevitable retribution. These bloody things are actually known locally as 'Lucky Beans'.

Two days later it was my turn to pretend I knew something about mechanics, and I lay under the Land Rover bashing things about with spanner and hammer as best I could. The task Chris had given me was to 'sort out'- the exhaust pipe. I had parked on a nice flat piece of grass near the bungalow and was laying face upwards with just my head peeping out trying to avoid dirt, filth, and rust getting into my eyes as I probed unknowingly and uselessly underneath the car with my hands.

All of a sudden I saw an upside-down Mr Smith approaching slowly and deliberately and with that sort of smile only dogs can portray although looking more comic being 180 degrees in the obverse. I was not scared as despite his reputation he was a loving dog if you were not one of the many million or so members of our species he was not prepared to tolerate; but feeling trapped under the car with little room for manoeuvre, and with there being no-one else around I thought it best to stay inert and not breathe. 'Good dog' I thought, sending him some mental waves; 'There's a good boy, I am your best friend, off you go now, go and kill some monkeys! Look why don't you just F*** off, no actually I love you, good dog.' Mr Smith was not fooled, Mr Smith was determined, the vibes were not getting through, and the doggy smile turned into a wicked doggy grin. He approached.

For the first time, being upside down, I noticed that this white monster of a dog was not all white at all. Hanging at the rear of him were two huge oval shaped dark dusky pink testicles with black shiny hats. All I could think of were giant lucky beans as Mr Smith reversed himself onto my head and sat heavily on my face, a boiling hot lucky bean nestled comfortably in each of my eye sockets.

At the top of Zomba mountain is a plateau and a hotel called the Kuchawe Inn. We were drinking in the bar one night when we met a charming middle-aged couple called Joan and Fred who lived at the bottom of the mountain. Fred was a jovial and somewhat stout character in Pickwickian fashion originally from the English Midlands but who nevertheless commanded respect, and Joan was another charming lady who wanted to mother us. The hotel itself was small and fabulously situated but lacked a swimming pool which we were informed was disallowed as the mountain was infested with leopard which would otherwise use the pool as their own bar and restaurant. In fact, every night both going up and back down the steep sheer-sided road from the Inn we would catch leopard in our headlights, and unintentionally chase them until there was some platform from which they could leap to safety into the thick forest – it was not a place to break down.

Needless to say we went to stay with this lovely couple once Jimmy was on his feet again. Fred and Joan had a nice bungalow surrounded by a wire fence connected to the mains as they had been burgled once and had decided to fry any further transgressors. They also had a security guard every evening to patrol the garden. The unfortunates who undertook this role were probably paid a pittance and had to walk many miles to get to the house before their night's work even began. Consequently whenever we got back from our evening's entertainment the guard was always asleep on duty. Fred would always steal the guard's hat before bedtime and sneak gigglingly away to await the outcome. Inevitably there would be a timid tap on the window a couple of hours later and a forlorn but hatless guard would be invited in to tell his story. In most instances a large crowd of bad men had tried to get into the house and after a big fight the guard had won but only after being knocked unconscious and losing his hat. Sometimes animals had flown over the fence and stolen the hat – we imagined griffins or pterodactyls. Once, the guard had seen off a whole pride of lions but had lost his hat into the bargain. They were all always amazed and delighted when Fred eventually gave their hat back (they would have been sacked if they had really lost it), but always swore they had not been asleep, stuck by their stories, but at least remained   a little more diligent until morning.

We fell in love with our life in this little haven of Africa and on learning that Joan was a Cordon Bleu cook and that the Kuchawe Inn was for sale we decided to club together our resources, buy it, and make our fortune as hoteliers. This may sound like a pipedream but in fact I have always believed you can do anything if you put your mind to it.

Within days I had put together all the bones of a business plan using Fred's typewriter; all we needed was money, permission (we were foreigners in transit) and some sound financial projections.

The latter we based on the hotel's current books, information from other friendly locals and the conviction that using our contacts in the UK and southern Africa we could attract a wealthy clientele. The one disturbing

113

aspect of going through the books was the very high staff turnover. This turned out to be due to a Zomba Palace ruling that forbade staff other than management to stay in the hotel overnight as it was situated above, and looked down upon the palace complex. Consequently the staff would walk down the mountain to their village each evening, at the mercy of the infestation of leopard, many of which were rabid. We estimated that if we took the trouble to drive them down each evening we could feed a lot less leopard, save at least thirty lives a year and greatly improve staff morale!

Permission was effectively down to the palace liking our business plan and us raising the money. The money I achieved through a loan from the Malawi Development Bank, somehow raising a quarter of a million pounds on the basis that my father would back this with twenty-five thousand pounds worth of Swiss Francs (in a numbered Swiss bank account). Too good to be true? Welcome to Africa.

Within a week I was asked to submit my passport to the palace as I was going to be made a temporary citizen, and a date was set for me to meet the right-hand lady of the President of Malawi who would introduce me to my fellow Directors – a bunch of local tribal chiefs who would enjoy the benefit of our labours and add no value. It turned out that my plan had been too good and had attracted interest at the highest level! It was only now that someone whispered in my ear an interesting story. Had I heard the one about the Englishman who had built up a good business, attracted lots of foreign investment, and when the profits were about to come to fruition had been given twenty-four hours to get out of the country? His successful business became a subsidiary of Press Industries, an operation with a surprisingly diverse portfolio, and reputed to be owned by the President himself. It was time to disappear once again.

Within seventy-six hours I said goodbye to all my friends with a very nice send-off at Blantyre airport; I waved farewell to Chobe the Land Rover which I had given away, and which was destined to become an ambulance, and I flew back to Zimbabwe. Within a further three months my African adventure was over. I left that wonderful black continent, supposed birthplace of all our ancestors, with a feeling of emptiness only sad songs can infuse; that only First World War poets can come near to portraying in words; and that scientists have *no* words for. But I was heading back to the UK and the bosom of my family, accompanied by a young lady who would also become a wife albeit for a while, but who would give me the two most beautifully special daughters that ever came out of any story-book still to be written – Alex and Tiff!

It is a late December morning and bitterly cold and dark outside, which is why for once I am appreciating the new style carriages that have heaters that actually heat, fixed windows that can't be left ajar, and doors that only slide open if someone wants to embark or alight. Incredibly, I am now into the second year of my studies and despite my meandering mind, finding that I am beginning to learn something and thoroughly enjoying doing my degree. At school I hardly ever did my homework; now I do it all. At school I rarely turned up on a Saturday (which you were definitely supposed to); now I go regularly. At school I failed all my exams; now I am near the top of the class and pass them all. At school I hated most of the teachers; now most of my tutors have become friends. As I have always played the fool and got up to mischief in my working life, perhaps my parents should have put me into employment at age seven (when I don't think anyone would have noticed much difference in my behaviour), and organised for me to officially start school in my late forties. Mind you, I must have really liked school at one stage, because that fact actually saved my life!

*I was eleven years old, and my parents were busy organising our annual summer holiday. I remember them consulting me, because the dates they wanted to book meant I would have to go straight back to school afterwards, leaving me no time to prepare for the all important 11+ exam. I naturally put my foot down at this affront and flatly refused to go, being extremely stubborn; set in my ways; and well deserving of the previously mentioned title 'little Hitler', which was more than appropriate because they were planning to take us to Austria. This visit to the 'Little Corporal's' homeland had been deliberately selected, because the year before we had holidayed in Belgium, and us three boys had behaved so badly, Dad had curtailed the vacation, and angrily brought us home in disgrace a week early. Austria however, filled my father with fresh confidence by providing him with the ultimate Teutonic sword of Damocles to hold over us – **lederhosen!** If we misbehaved this time, not only would we be made to wear these dreadful leather instruments of torture and acute embarrassment whilst on holiday, he additionally threatened to make us wear them to school upon our return; and we believed him.*

Anyhow, I had won my case, and we were staying in the little Tyrolean village of Seefeld a week earlier than my parents would have ideally liked. The first seven days of this vacation were a complete joy, what with sweet young girls wearing national costume and Heidi hairstyles to fall in love with; old ladies sitting outside quaint chocolate box chalets to make faces at; delicious fruit filled cakes and pastries to munch by the

117

bag-full; chairlifts and cable cars to play on; cows with bells to chase; a big rock strewn glacier to walk across despite it being mid-summer; schnapps to take covert sips of when the parents weren't paying attention, and we were even having great fun pretending to be the Von Trapp family albeit without any girls, running about the hills holding hands in a daisy chain fashion, and mother bringing them alive by singing her heart out. Week two however, seemed oddly strange by comparison. For one thing the hotel was only half full with some guests having gone home but no new guests having arrived, and the villagers seemed to have become withdrawn, with some shops and cafes even closing for no apparent reason. To liven and cheer things up, my parents suggested we escape the valley for a while and take a coach trip through the twisty windy alpine roads to visit Germany. But once again I donned my jackboots and refused to go on the grounds I would be violently car-sick on such a journey (I was very prone to motion sickness at that age), and I remained immovable on the subject. So I think we did some more hill singing instead, whilst searching for nuns who might look like Julie Andrews (who incidentally went to the same school as me, but a thousand years earlier). But the following day, if anything, the whole village seemed in even more sombre a mood, and it was only on the final day of our holiday we finally learnt from the apologetic and tearful manager of our hostelry, what had befallen this tiny community.

First of all, the plane we should have been on if I hadn't insisted on advancing the holiday by a week due to school, had crashed. The aircraft was a little 'British Eagle' Vickers Viscount that had experienced catastrophic engine failure, and the brave pilot had tried to land on a German autobahn but had run out of road, ending up hitting a bridge; and everyone had been killed thus explaining the lack of any new guests in the hotel. Secondly, the coach we would have been on through the twisty windy alpine roads if I hadn't insisted on not going, had experienced catastrophic driver failure and fallen off a cliff; and everyone had been killed, including some tourists from the village.

Now strangely enough, my father had had a strong premonition that something was going to go wrong in relation to this holiday, and for the first time ever had taken the precaution of informing the police that we were going away (something you were supposed to do in those days to maintain the validity of your home insurance policy). So we returned home from this holiday (via Germany and a different type of aircraft), somehow having sidestepped fate twice (thanks to me), and having narrowly avoided being forced into lederhosen a few dozen times (thanks to the intervention of Mother), but only to discover we had been burgled, with the thieves evidently having been living in our house for many days whilst they ransacked the place. The police had suspiciously failed to notice anything suspicious themselves whilst on their daily patrol, despite the evidence of many broken windows, and my father certainly felt he had more than tempted fate by advising the police in the first place. So no-one in my family has ever advised the police about anything, ever

*again; I did pass my 11+ exam despite everything; oh,
and playing anything from the 'Sound of Music' film was
banned in our house thereafter, Mother's vinyl copy of
the soundtrack being one of the few records the thieves
(probably deliberately) omitted to break.*

Completely relevant to my glacier trekking
reminiscences, today I am learning all about the Great
Ice Age, a period of Earth's history that we are actually
in the middle of. It seems that in its many billion years
of existence, the Earth has shifted between 'Greenhouse'
conditions with no ice-caps, high temperatures, and
much higher sea-levels; to 'Ice-house' conditions with
the globe pretty well smothered in hundreds of metres of
thick ice, looking like a giant snowball. The Great Ice
Age, despite its name, is a sort of in-between state, split
into glacial and inter-glacial periods. The good thing for
me is that we are currently enjoying interglacial
conditions (despite the fact we do have glaciers), which
is why my nice garden by the sea in Southern England is
not tundra, but we should by rights be moving into a
glacial period (where we will have even more and much
bigger glaciers), and where I swap my bucket and spade
for crampons and an ice-pick. Thankfully, man-made
global warming has apparently put the brakes on this
trend for the time being, although with what ultimate
consequences remains to be seen.

We have stopped at a station, and I look up from
my book because I feel an icy shiver as the doors slide
open to let in an old lady, accompanied by a blast of cold

morning air. If my coat and scarf were not tucked up asleep on the rack above my head, I would certainly sink into them for comfort. As it is, I turn up my collar and draw my shoulders together in an unconscious attempt to retain body heat. It is definitely not the sort of day you would want to hang your head out of the train window; especially just for fun...

EXTREMELY NAUGHTY BOYS

I had returned safely from my African venture, and was commuting from Horley, south of London, to London Bridge station on a daily basis. I was working in the London Insurance Market for the same insurance broker as my elder brother, who had returned from his venture in America; but although he lived in the same road as myself and caught the same train (once again the 7.52 to London Bridge!), we were not on speaking terms due to differences between our respective wives, and their cognisance of the fact that whenever my brother and I were together, it would end in mayhem. We would even stand on opposite ends of the platform every morning.

By evening however, the relationship had generally changed. For some reason, either one or both of us would have had a memorable luncheon involving such friends as Comrade Smirnoff, General Gordon or Monsieur Chardonnay, and would need assistance back to London Bridge station to prepare for the journey homewards. Sometimes these lunches involved so many friends and comrades that an afternoon escape was in order. Fortunately the company we worked for wisely utilised large revolving electronic filing systems called 'Lektrievers'. These were ceiling height, about two metres wide and consisted of a series of double ranked shelves of coffin size that revolved waterwheel fashion when the shelf you required was dialled up on the keypad. Files were kept on these shelves in strict alphabetic order and to be frank it was an efficient system. To be even more frank it was a great place to be hidden if you were so drunk you needed to be kept away from management for the afternoon. Kind friends would lay you down on a rarely used shelf e.g. closed claim files S-Z, then send you to the back of the machine for a well earned nap. This did take some getting used to, for if you woke up and panicked it was literally like having been buried alive and there was no escape until someone came to your rescue. If you were genuinely trying to work however, and urgently needed a file, it was particularly disconcerting as you waited for your selected shelf to arrive, to see seemingly dead colleagues rise from the depths and pass upwards as if on their way to that great wine bar in the sky.

As with most large City-based insurance companies, there were of course some unofficial ground rules you were expected to follow and which were drummed into you on your first day. At my company these included:-

Rule 1

Try not to go back to the office if you have had six pints of bitter, two bottles of red wine, a glass of port and a large gin to drink at lunchtime. Most especially try and avoid going back for a late afternoon important meeting with grumpy senior members of staff who have no sense of humour.

Rule 2

If you need a new pencil or biro, do not waste time dealing with the boring old fart in charge of stationery who will demand to see a pencil stub or empty biro tube. Wait until after hours, then rip the locked door off the stationery cupboard and help yourself and your friends to anything you want, filling your pockets if possible – but leave a polite thank-you note for the old fart to treasure.

Rule 3

If you are dealing with an important and complex insurance claim worth many thousands of pounds - you are completely out of your depth, beginning to get stressed, and don't want to let on you have effectively achieved nothing for the past two months – throw the claims file off London Bridge into the Thames on your way to the station on a Friday evening. Then have a wonderfully relaxed weekend.

Rule 4

If you have been asked to leave the company for any reason possibly associated with any of the above rules, don't forget to throw ALL your important work off London Bridge into the Thames on your way home.

As my brother was older than me and therefore had a larger expense account, many afternoons I would be called upon to dial him up and get him out of the building before he could realise his full potential for havoc. We would somehow tumble our way across London Bridge to London Bridge station, find our waiting train and of course, enter the buffet car where the ever smiling buffet attendant was ready to introduce us to new liquid friends. If we missed the train, London Bridge station had a wonderful buffet of its own, staffed by large and jolly beaming-faced West Indian ladies. Somehow they knew exactly how to make a pink gin (you throw out the angostura bitters) and a couple of these would steady us nicely for the journey home. Pink gin had become a favourite as both my brother and I had joined the Territorial Army, had been somehow identified as being potential officers and consequently reinvented ourselves as such, revelling in all the pomp and show.

Once aboard the train and suitably fuelled, we would work our way down the wonderful corridor carriages, and find somewhere appropriately concealed to lounge, lizard style.

Even though these were twelve coach trains, they were made up of three sets of four carriages, each of which had a driver's cab at each end. Quite by chance it so happened that a Chubb door key used correctly could open the locks to these cabs. Inside could be found two convenient and comfortable revolving seats; a dash board consisting of interesting and irresistible knobs and switches; and a couple of shelves of useful goodies such as explosive charges for use on the track to stop other trains in fog if there was an emergency. These latter items could be detonated by throwing a brick at them and were powerful enough to do considerable damage - apparently. Although you couldn't go into the front cab of course because the real driver was in there, or indeed the rear cab where the guard was usually based, you could turn the train lights on and off; blow the horn lots and lots of times; and say 'hello' to the driver and guard through the intercom – which always came as a bit of a shock to them both. Whilst the guard was running in a mad panic through the train to find which cab we were in and stop our fun, we would exit our cab, stand nicely and innocently in our smart business suits until he/she went by, then go to the now empty cab at the rear of the train, where we had the additional advantage of a rear view as we sped on our journey, hooting the horn for all it was worth. To avoid having our enjoyment curtailed, where the sets of four carriages joined there was a big heavy yellow door which was opened inwards to create a passageway thereby making up a longer train, or closed tightly shut and bolted if this was the front or rear cab. Once past the guard we could close one of these yellow doors behind us trapping the guard in the front part of the train and cutting off the guard's route through to us. What fun to sit glass in hand, watching the parallel lines of the track disappear to a distant point, and seeing all the interesting railway paraphernalia race past.

Just once, we were in just such a situation on a very wintry Christmas Eve having spent the afternoon celebrating in a wine bar, and we decided the rearward view, although spectacular with snow drifting across the tracks, was insufficient reward for such a festive occasion. We therefore opened the big rear yellow door of the train.

At the time we were probably travelling at about 90 mph and as we struggled to pull the heavy door inwards, the icy wind plucked hard at our clothes. The noise of the train became one long roar as the wheels thundered over the rails which narrowed away from us into the distant twilight. And, as complete idiots do, we dared each other to step outside. Above the train buffers and the central coupling there was a narrow ledge just wide enough to get half a step on, but all there was to hold on to was a grime-smeared vacuum pipe and a small metal hand rail, itself held on by two small loose screws. Above these however and at head height, was a sturdy looking window wiper on either side of the doorway, so gripping onto these we both somehow managed to manoeuvre ourselves outside, swivel round to face the rear, and ended up each sitting astride a massive buffer. Clutching with all our might onto the vacuum pipes and metal handrails behind us, we both sat in this death defying position, kicking our legs in thin air just above the level of the tracks. We looked at each other in disbelief and I know the madness I felt was fully reflected in my brother's eyes. Then we started screaming, both with exhilaration, and sheer terror at what we were doing.

Very soon the train tore through Purley station where we could see startled and alarmed station staff pointing at us and yelling, then the train hit some sets of points which shook it from side to side and made my teeth rattle in my head. By now I felt completely sober, massively dehydrated and sick with fear. I knew I was literally inches from death and as stuck in my position as the proverbial kid with his 'head through the railings'. If anything, the train seemed to have sped up and the track and the trees to the side were passing in a blur.

The train thundered into a railway cutting with towering walls on either side, shutting out what little light there had been, and casting a deep gloom over the snow-laden scene. Despite being frozen to the marrow, I was sweating profusely and beginning to really panic. I was losing my grip on the vacuum pipe and had visions of the screws working their way loose on the handrail. I saw my brother turn to look at me and could tell he was in a similar petrified state. This was no longer fun and I wished so hard it was all a dream.

The walls of the cutting grew even higher and seemed to meet overhead making me feel insignificant and very vulnerable. Now the train raced past a long disused signal-box, the sole sentinel before the mouth of the mile long Merstham tunnel. If ever there was a sight to conjure up Dickensian ghosts from a Christmas past, it was that lonely and long forgotten signal-box, somehow lit as if from within by a last failing ray of winter sun – I could even imagine a spectral voice from the roof of the cutting calling 'Helloa, below there!' I know I had tears in my eyes.

The cacophony of noise became deafening as we entered the pitch blackness of the tunnel, I stared mesmerised as the entrance to the tunnel reduced to a tiny dot and then disappeared before my eyes. The steel wheels on the steel rails screamed as we rattled and shook; sparks sprayed from beneath the train illuminating the shiny track in an orange hue. Occasionally there would be an explosion of electric blue sparks from the third rail – the scaring conductor rail which carries the power. When this happened the tunnel would be lit for a split-instant creating monstrous shadows, and tainting the air with a thick metallic burning smell on top of the damp sooty aroma left over from a century of steam trains. After less than a minute of this overpowering, mind-numbing experience we had both had enough, this was the stuff supposed to be reserved for nightmares. The freezing buffers were slippery with thick grease, we were numb with cold, our arms ached from holding on for dear life, and we had both had visions of the big yellow door slamming shut and leaving us trapped outside to a hideous fate. Even worse was the thought that a train would come the other way, tear past our train with only inches to spare, and suck us off our precarious perch either to be cut to pieces under the wheels, or skinned alive and torn to ribbons as we were dragged dangling behind. But somehow - I will never know how, we were suddenly back in the warm rear cab with its friendly subdued glow of light, the big yellow door was slammed shut against the horror outside, and we stood staring at each other and then hugging each other with relief.

Without needing to say anything, we both walked as far up the train to the front as possible (remember, we had closed off half the train to shut out the guard), and tidied ourselves up as best we could as the train slowed down for Horley station.

Obviously the onlookers at Purley had passed the word, and at Horley the train was met by the station master, a few more station staff, and lots of Police. As we had expected however, they were grouped at the back of the train ready to pounce on and arrest two young idiot hooligans. The last people they suspected were two serious looking, smartly dressed, pin-striped businessmen, alighting from the train a few carriages from the rear, and thankfully with thick black winter coats hiding the mass of grease on their nice suit trousers which inevitably ended up in the dustbin. Only the young yob-like ticket inspector (who recognised a drunk when he saw one), grinned knowingly at us and chuckled to himself as we passed out of the station. After all – It was Christmas. And at home, I had waiting for me my very first little daughter, who would be waking up the next morning to open her own, very first little train-set, from Santa. And, if she was really lucky, she could even watch me play with it in complete safety!

It is another evening journey and I am on the Hastings line again, travelling back down to my home in Rudyard Kipling country. When I first started journeying on this line I had a natural fear of falling asleep and missing my station; instead, ending up in the sidings at the end of the line. I say natural fear because I have done this so often over the years, I must have visited most station termini on the whole South coast of England. There is a fundamental combination of forces behind these escapades, and that is working in insurance in the City, and alcohol. Perhaps the worst time was quite recent, with me ending up at Hastings station one very, very cold winter's evening on the last train of the night, having spent all my money, lost my coat somewhere, and having left my wallet at home. Being very much the worse for wear, all I could think of was finding a place to rest my head, then hopefully catching the first train out in the morning to the station I had sailed through earlier in my unconscious state.

Being 'down and out in Hastings' doesn't have the romantic cachet of the Parisian version; all I could find was a lonely bench on the seashore, well away from other homeless humanity who might want to play at swapping clothes with me, or borrow my briefcase. As what I now recognise as advanced hypothermia started

132

to set in, my only drunken solution was to huddle into a ball on the pebble beach, shiver uncontrollably, and watch the frost slowly materialise on my body. Inside the case I was clutching close to my chest was a large and thick geology book, which in retrospect I could have used as padding for warmth; and that, had I had the inclination to read at the time, could have told me a lot about the very beach I was lying on.

150 million years ago, Hastings was a series of lagoons, lakes and rivers; with colourful, feathered, but sober dinosaurs marching merrily around. Then, some millions of years later as the Earth heated up and the ice caps melted away, the sea level rose and invaded the land, and the chalk for which much of the south coast of England is famous was laid down. This chalk is made from the skeletal remains of an incalculable number of tiny creatures that lived in those seas; remains which can be clearly seen under a powerful microscope. Nested in amongst the exposed chalk in the cliffs we see today, are black bands of flint nodules; the sort of rocks primitive man used to make arrow heads and spears from; which heralded a famous cartoon series; which my house is made from; and many of which ended up as stones on Hastings beach. Flint as you may know is extremely hard, but actually has its origin in the remains of those softest of creatures - sponges. Well I certainly wasn't lying on a sponge bed, and remarkably discovering myself still alive in the early hours, I also found my face full of awkward and painful dents from my pebble pillow. Arriving ticketless at Hastings station shortly afterwards, hoping to catch a free ride on the train home,

I could clearly see in the eyes of the disbelieving ticket inspector as I explained my sorry tale that from my dishevelled, haggard, unshaven, face-dented, and damp and filthy suited state, I had finally hit rock bottom (excuse the geological pun), and horror of horrors, taken on the mantle of my nemesis - the 'Unlikely Gentleman!'

On the South coast of England there is a wonderful little railway, which despite having been visited by my brothers and I, is still providing pleasure to thousands of adults and children every year. The Romney, Hythe and Dymchurch Railway (RH&DR), runs a fleet of fabulous steam engines, each of which is a third the size of a full scale engine (so about three foot high), but powerful enough to pull a train of at least a hundred or so people. During the early war years the little engines even towed armour plated anti-aircraft guns back and forth along the coast as part of our defence against the expected German invasion.

At one end of the seventy-six year old railway is Hythe station. Hythe is one of the five 'Cinque' ports set up by Edward the Confessor to protect Saxon Britain from invasion by a different enemy at the time, the French, and was more firmly established a couple of hundred years later by another Edward - Longshanks. He is the charming King who beat up the Scots so terribly, and who enjoyed throwing an obvious 'Friend of Dorothy' out of the castle window in the film *Braveheart*. Hythe station was also the site of a small disaster when one of the steam engines called 'Hercules', crashed through the buffers and smashed its way into the station car-park. Many years after this event however, and one complete rebuild later for this brave little red engine, I had the great fortune to experience one of every schoolboy's dreams and travel the full thirteen mile length of the railway in Hercules' small but cosy cab, something King George VI had similarly enjoyed.

One of my father's clients was a proper member of the gentry and like me, also called Julian. Posh Julian lived in a fairy tale castle in Somerset and was interested in buying the railway as a tax efficient investment. He and my dad had been invited to view and experience the prospective purchase, and it being November and out of season, the railway had opened up especially for them. With Paul now based in the U.S. and Timmy now sadly no longer with us, I got to take an 'official' day off school (I was taking a lot of unofficial days off school at the time, but my parents were unaware of this) and I got to go too!

It takes almost as long to get an RH&DR engine fired up as its full-sized cousins, so only Hercules was in steam that day, although the railway had put on the royal coach for the occasion, so we all felt very special and privileged. I suspect that Posh Julian always felt very special and privileged but that is by the by. In fact, I had by far the best of things, because I got to drive the train; endlessly toot the whistle; play as fireman stoking the boiler; and experience all the sights, sounds and smells from the deliciously warm cab as we sped through all the stations, whilst the others just talked business in the cold as they rattled along in the tiny royal coach. As Posh Julian didn't buy the railway in any event, I could tell he was a little resentful of me. He did however invite us back to stay at his castle with him, where we were joined by Mum and Mrs Posh Julian, and a pack of gundogs as you would expect.

Dunster castle is quite magnificent, had been in the Posh Julian family since thirteen hundred and something, but nowadays belongs to the National Trust and is open to the public. Although it is called and looks like a castle in every sense with its towers and turrets, Dunster lacks battlements and is only therefore 'officially' a fortress as explained by Posh Julian. It also sadly lacks a dungeon and torture chamber, the first intelligence I sought on seeing this mighty edifice. Once through the 14th Century gatehouse and into the main courtyard, we entered the castle building through the ancient oak and iron front doors into a spacious baronial type hall complete with carved stone fireplace, and with broad staircases winding up each side. It being already time to freshen up and dress for dinner, we were led by an equally ancient and lop-sided servant to our rooms in an upstairs wing, it being made clear that the other wing was out of bounds to us:

'It being where the Master's mother is dying' this ghoulish character explained to us, giving me a particularly sideways and knowing leer.

Following 'Lurch' down a long and creaking corridor past historic family portraits, suits of armour, and tapestries countless centuries old, my parents were put into a capacious suite and I was taken to my own room much further down the corridor, off a dark and draughty passageway. The room was vast with almost another room leading off it separated by a twenty foot high medieval curtain, from where the single huge arched window looked out into woodland and a distant view of the cold grey winter ocean. The furniture consisted of just one immense and very old looking four poster bed with its own curtained walls, and a wash basin. Lurch explained without looking me in the eye, that as the electricity was suspect, at bedtime I would be given a candle to light my way to bed; that I should get into the four-poster and close the curtains for warmth; and that he would be on hand to; blow out the candle, close off the 'window room', and make all quiet 'so as not to wake the dead!' As he creaked away I had a deep sense of foreboding.

I quickly dressed in a pair of flares and a black velvet jacket with cravat (all the rage in the seventies) and as near to a Little Lord Fauntleroy outfit as I could manage, and set off to explore our wing. After some twenty minutes of peering in rooms without discovering anything of particular interest (or pocket-sized), I made my way downstairs to the main hall. Mother and Father were standing by the now raging fireplace with Mother helping herself to biscuits and little pieces of meat from a large silver bowl placed on a table nearby. A few minutes later a female hunch-backed version of Lurch appeared to call us in to dinner, but first took the silver bowl away from Mother, scowled at her, and then placed it on the floor for the dogs.

I don't remember much of dinner except that it was not very well cooked, but afterwards we all sat in Posh Julian's cosy warm library and had drinks. I of course was full of adolescent questions, and learnt that the bed I was to sleep in was used by King Charles II (the Merry Monarch no less – how appropriate) who stayed at the castle during the plague; that for centuries past the family had employed all the people in the village otherwise unemployable due to deformity or madness; but that the castle was not haunted, or at least not by anything we should be unnecessarily worried about. My parents and I glanced at each other knowingly. Needless to say after this revelation I kept glancing at the gold carriage clock on Posh Julian's desk, thinking of the cold, dark, lonely room that awaited me, and hoping bedtime would never come around. It was quite strange to be sitting in what was effectively a museum, surrounded by countless historic and priceless items, any one of which would be highly regarded on a television antique show but which were collectively taken for granted, not seen as being valuable but as belonging to the old castle as they always had done, and always would. Becoming immune to the muted conversation around me as time ticked on, I fell into a quiet reverie.

As always happens, the hands on the golden clock crept round to midnight, somebody unhelpfully said it was past the 'witching hour', and Mrs Posh Julian saw us upstairs into my parent's room, handing me a 'Willy Winky' candle before she bade us goodnight and floated away. I asked Dad was he scared and he laughed and said,

'No, I'm not on my own, I'm sleeping with your mother'.

And so with candle in hand, I reluctantly made my way down the long, long dark passageway towards where I thought my own room was. Unfortunately I had spent too much time exploring before dinner and was now disorientated. I consequently had to open numerous doors and peer into the dark rooms until my candle and the faint winter moonlight slowly revealed the contents inside. The rooms were either stark and empty, or contained furniture draped in white dust-sheets, the shapes of which in the subdued light started creating increasingly ghostly visions in my mind. In fact the word **ghost** loomed ever larger in my thoughts. The further I went the more lost I got, and the more doors I opened, the more I could feel myself being watched. It was as if someone or something was looking over my shoulder; I could even sense their presence which made my skin prickle. All the while the wind through the passage was making a thousand strange whispering and rustling sounds, and although I kept looking behind me, and once or twice span quickly round, I didn't hear or see anyone or anything.

At last having retraced my steps I opened a door I must have missed and recognised with relief my own room on seeing my overnight bag. The room was especially dark and cold and I could see that the big curtain had been closed shutting off any chance of light from the window room. Also, one of the curtains in the four poster had been left open for me with the sheets turned back. The candle began to gutter in the cold air and grow dim so I quickly shrugged off my clothes and dived onto the high bed, taking the candle with me and shutting the bed curtain behind me. I sat with my knees up to my chest and the covers pulled around me, one arm holding my candle above the heavy bedspread, casting a glow on the canopy above. Once I had calmed down and shivered myself warm, I settled back and began to relax and feel safer, thinking this is the exact spot where a young King slept hundreds of years ago. I could smell and sense the history surrounding me and felt quite cocooned in my small space.

Then I heard noises. I could distinctly hear something or someone moving in the room and whether it was my imagination or not, the atmosphere became very oppressive, and then the sound abruptly ceased. I dared to open the bed curtain a crack to see if there was any light in the room but it was pitch black outside so I quickly closed it again and began to shake with fright, all the time listening intently. My cocoon began to feel more like a coffin and I shrank away from the curtain walls not wanting to be connected to the room outside, or to touch something with so much unknown history attached. I thought again of that King and wondered if he had had people beheaded or cruelly tortured to death as punishment for killing his father, Charles I. I imagined a headless twisted man in old fashioned clothes and a wide blood-soaked collar, blindly stalking the room out for revenge, and feeling for the bed and his intended victim with big horribly disfigured and smashed hands. Then I heard the noise again. With my senses on full alert, I definitely heard someone or something breathing heavily from behind the big window curtain, the swish of the drape being pulled back and then the sound of something being slowly and deliberately dragged along the wooden floor towards my bed. I was petrified, I wanted to shout out but was too scared to even do that. I think I made some inadvertent yelping sounds, and I know I had tears running down my cheeks and that I was shaking. Then the curtains by my head *burst* open; a huge, terrifying face appeared evilly illuminated by the candle flame, and Lurch blew my candle out. As he stomped away, chuckling to himself, I hid my head under the covers and rocked myself to sleep. I was so relieved I might have wet myself.

Five munchkin-sized stations further along the coast from Hythe, is a station that used to be called

Maddiesons Camp at the town of Greatstone. A few years before the abovementioned experience, my parents took my brothers and I, and a friend of Paul's for a week's holiday in a rented house by the sea at Greatstone. This was the first time we came across the little railway which ran conveniently past the back of the house, and we could sit in the back garden and watch the trains steam past every hour or so. As can be imagined the railway was an instant magnet for us and we would spend many an hour listening out for the high pitched ringing on the track which meant a train was coming; guessing which engine it would be of the dozen or so which the RH&DR ran; putting pennies on the track for the engines to squash flat, and waving to the trains as children do. Unfortunately these many hours of innocent fun only amounted up to one whole day before as usual, my elder brother became bored.

At the time, one of our favourite films was *Hannibal Brooks* starring our favourite actor Oliver Reed. This is an adventure set in Germany during World War 2, where Reed is a British prisoner working at Munich Zoo, who escapes during an air raid, and makes it to freedom creating much mayhem for the Germans along the way. In one memorable part of the film, Reed has teamed up with some weirdo partisans far better suited to some drug-crazed Vietnamese war movie, and they, together with the help of an Indian elephant Reed earlier liberated from the zoo, manage to push lots of logs onto a railway line to stop a trainload of tanks, which they then blow up. They then get chased by some very irate German soldiers, led by an even angrier and nasty officer who threatens to personally kill them if they are caught.

Oliver Reed had at his disposal for this escapade a whole host of heavily armed partisans; some explosive; and one huge brown Indian elephant called Lucy. My brother had at his disposal one teenager; two little boys; and one very soppy yellow dog called Thunder. Nevertheless we managed to manoeuvre a heavy tree trunk across the railway track late that evening, and secreted ourselves in nearby bushes the following morning to see if we would stop the first train to go by, which would of course be towing a cargo of imaginary tanks and full of German soldiers. The thought that we might derail the train and cause untold misery never occurred to us - this was war! When we did in fact manage to bring the train to a screeching and hissing halt, we were so surprised at the enormity of what we had done, we stood up from our hiding place in a very un-soldierlike fashion and so giving our position away, and only to be shouted at by horrified and irate passengers (none of whom sounded German to me) and chased by a very big, very angry driver who threatened to personally kill us if he caught us, and probably meant it.

As a beach resort, Greatstone doesn't have any sand except at very low tide and far out towards the sea. I know this because on the first morning I was trapped in quicksand up to my neck and had to be rescued by men with planks and rope. Instead the beaches are awash with pebbles. Consequently, we were able to easily convince

Mum and Dad that far more appropriate holiday toys to buy us at the local shop than buckets and spades, were of course catapults.

Now as any boy who has ever had an air-rifle will know only too well, it is simply a matter of time before your eye strays from the boring paper bulls-eye you are supposed to be aiming at, and starts exploring for more exciting and reactive targets. So too with catapults! How many times can you hit a tin can, or see how far you can send a stone before someone is bound to come up with a better idea?

A couple of gardens away from our house stood the afore-mentioned Maddiesons Camp. This was a holiday camp in true Butlin's style only on a far smaller scale.

We knew all about such camps having spent most of our early childhood holidays at such venues. The first of these that I remember was in Norfolk called Caister Camp, and I must have been about three years old. Upon arrival, I recall that all the family were given animal badges to wear at all times. We were proudly designated as Lions, and this meant we ate with other Lions in the Lions area of the giant army style canteen; cheered when any Lions achieved anything of note and we were told to cheer; chanted L.I.O.N.S. LIONS when we were told to chant; teamed up with other Lions in the compulsory sporting events; and naturally picked on any kids who didn't sport a Lions badge. I think the management of that establishment must have had a wicked sense of humour because all the fat people (who were rare at the time) were given Hippo badges to wear.

There were a lot of hippos staying at Maddiesons Camp that summer, most of whom were elderly females wallowing in sun loungers next to the small outside paddling pool. Paul sent my little brother Timmy and I into the camp to play in the pool alongside the other small children, which seems innocuous enough, but I had been tasked with a special covert mission. This was to be another military operation, and I was to be the forward observation post for my brother and his friend's artillery position based in our garden.

We knew it was forbidden and could be very dangerous to fire stones at people with our catapults. Firing stones high into the air 'blind' however, mortar style, without actually aiming at anyone in particular was considered far more sporting and therefore perfectly acceptable. What the artillery needed though was feedback on how near to the fat targets their 'shells' were landing. And so the bombardment began.

I would watch and try and spot the trajectory of incoming stones and mentally work out the height and therefore strength of each shot in relation to the impact zone. This was all quite sophisticated and within minutes of racing back and forth with my information, the creeping barrage worked its way steadily towards the fat sleeping targets, with the missiles thudding into the grass or crashing off the roofs of the chalets. But one target was wide awake. This lady was sitting up, wearing large horn rimmed glasses which gave her massive round eyes, and keenly observing everything happening in and around the pool. If the other ladies were hippos this one was a large croc, waiting for her chance to pounce, and she had me in her sights.

The first direct hit thumped into a lady's bulbous tummy making her podgy arms and legs bounce upwards and brought forth a loud squeal, and much giggling from Timmy and I. A second hit a few moments later had a similar bouncing limb effect on a different lady who made a sound like gas escaping from a large zeppelin airship. A deal of confusion followed amongst the now awake ladies, and a loud discussion ending with seagulls dropping stones being blamed as the most likely culprits. The next few shots were misses and the croc watched with suspicious interest as I ran to the camp entrance and back again to report my analysis. A further direct hit had a different effect on the ladies from the others. There were no seagulls to be seen in the vicinity, but what could quite clearly be seen were two guilty looking little boys in the paddling pool, one of whom (me) was still holding in a massive laughing fit resulting from the previous direct hit. I could feel the croc's eyes boring into me and she saw me glance towards the camp entrance. To make things worse, somehow sensing that the fun was to be imminently curtailed, the calibre of the missiles my brother was using (which up to now had been small), increased markedly as did the rate of fire. As a consequence, the shelling became erratic and distinctly dangerous. Suddenly the croc made her move. She pointed at me and screamed:

'It was him! He's to blame!' and started calling for the camp commandant. It was high time for our new model army to make a hasty retreat.

We were doing well! It was only day two of our holiday; we were banned from the beach in case I got stuck again; we daren't go near the railway in case the angry driver recognised us; and the camp was clearly out of bounds. It was going to feel like a long week with our military activities so summarily curtailed. But unbeknown to my elder brother and I at the time, we would return to this piece of coast in a 'real' military capacity some twenty years later.

The final station on the RH&DR line is Dungeness where the line loops round some quaint old fishing huts set amongst the shingle, any of which would have provided an ideal base for a young David Copperfield. This mystical-sounding and lonely part of Kent is also home to two lighthouses (one new, one old), a lifeboat station, lots of rare fauna, a nuclear power-station, some pre-radar 'Listening Ears' and lots of Ministry of Defence land.

I was in my late twenties, my brother was in his early thirties, and we had just joined the Territorial Army, and looking back, something we should have been forced to become involved with in our teens. This was to be our very first weekend away as soldiers, everything was new to us including our fellow 'brothers in arms', and we had no idea what to expect.

It was a Friday evening. We had assembled at our local drill hall with the rest of 'C' Company; been bundled into the back of a couple of draughty 'four tonner' trucks; and driven through the cold night air to some woods in the depths of Hampshire. Here we were ordered to get some rest in our bashers (for the uninitiated this is a poncho tied between two trees that you lay under in your sleeping bag, fully dressed, and cuddling your rifle) until morning, when manoeuvres would commence. As new recruits however, Paul and I were told we would be woken at four in the morning for our two-hour turn at sentry duty, which really meant keeping an eye on our company vehicles in the field nearby.

Kicked rudely awake at the appointed hour by an invisible person who had been on duty before us, we took our turn walking in opposite directions round the trucks and the officer's Land Rover, trying to stay awake, stave off boredom, and keep ourselves warm. Luckily I had thought to bring along a selection of spirit miniatures from my Dad's old collection, and so every time our paths crossed on our circuit we would stop and drink a Drambuie, or a Whisky, or a Cognac, or a Crème de Menthe, or a Port, or Schnapps. After about an hour of this, we were shaken out of our lethargy and alcohol induced fug by the unmistakable sound of helicopters. Sure enough in the early dawn sky we could see lights approaching and the sound of beating engines getting ever louder. To our amazement the lights quickly became two massive Puma army helicopters circling our field and looking for a convenient place to come down. As they landed right next to us we were nearly knocked over by the massive downdraft through which a very young, helmeted officer appeared, to confirm that we *were* actually 'C' Company Queens Regiment, and to inform us that this was to be our transport for the day! Assuming we were in command, he apologised that things had had to be moved forwards by two hours hence they were early, but we said it didn't matter; it was jolly nice of him to bring some helicopters with him anyway; and we shared a Cointreau with him.

As the engines died down and the rotors came to a halt, one of our own officers appeared and Paul and I were posted to a Puma each to stand guard whilst the rest of the Company were roused. I don't need to describe how excited I felt standing next to a real army helicopter; feeling like a real soldier myself; never having been in a helicopter before, and knowing we were going into 'action' in these incredible beasts.

As the Company assembled and made ready to embark, our Captain (who was a little bit camp) told Paul and I that as we had been on watch and had been so polite to the nice helicopter officer, we could be the last men aboard which would give us the best view.

Being last in an army helicopter meant that the machine was already more than a hundred feet up before you were properly inside, and that you then sat with your legs dangling from the fuselage and holding on for dear life as you sped through the air. This was pure exhilaration and just like being part of the helicopter gunship raid in the movie *Apocalypse Now*. Even better, I could see Paul sitting in the same position in his helicopter, and wearing a massive ear to ear smile on his face. We could even salute each other as the Pumas banked in formation.

Within twenty minutes we had reached the Kent coast. Looking down from a thousand feet I was amazed to recognise the line of the Romney Hythe and Dymchurch Railway running along beneath us. I signalled to Paul who had spotted the same, and sure enough our helicopters followed the route of the railway all the way to Dungeness. It was like having an aerial view of a Hornby train set. I could identify the little stations, the engine sheds, and trains of tiny carriages waiting patiently in the sidings. Half way along the line at New Romney station, there were even some engines being got into steam for the day ahead. This was indeed magical, and what an incredible introduction to the T.A.

Later that day we were to be further spoilt. Our Pumas had dropped us at Dungeness to play at being soldiers, and then flown off elsewhere. To take us back to our field that evening, we were to have a different treat – for there waiting for us was a Chinook!

Chinooks are huge twin rotor, troop transport helicopters still widely in use, and large enough to hold our entire Company of thirty, sitting facing each other on opposite sides of the fuselage. It had been a long and utterly exhausting day; running around on the shingle in full kit pretty well since daybreak; scrambling through dense gorse bushes; clambering over old walls and barbed wire fences, and covering countless miles in the process; and after just a few minutes in the air, most of the Company were fast asleep. The warm, dark interior of the Chinook; the humming of the engines; the smell of oil, grease, and aviation fuel; and the vibrating of the airframe; together with the massive elation of the day; all combined to have a most soporific effect. As I felt my eyelids drooping but before I too entered the world of dreams, I glanced about me and was vividly reminded of the final scene of my all-time favourite war film, *Where Eagles Dare*. All it needed was the sound of the drums at the start of the magnificent soundtrack…

I am wearing a large red rose in my lapel. Apart from when watching our national team play football, cricket or rugby, St George's seems to be the only day when it is politically correct to openly boast of being English. I have spent this afternoon at the St. George's Day Club luncheon in central London with my great friends Roger Foord and Melvyn Byrne (at Melvyn's kind invitation), and I am now on my way home. There was a time when most gentlemen would wear a buttonhole every day, but then there was a time when most gentlemen would wear a tie every day as well. A paper poppy is the only floral embellishment still seen regularly, marking the season when we all remember our military forebears and when we all feel that little bit more morally upright.

It was on Remembrance Day two years ago that there was a knock at the door of my home in Rudyard Kipling country, delivered by an elderly lady with two teenagers, all three smartly dressed in black and wearing real poppies. It turned out that they were in the village to pay respects at the war memorial, which listed amongst too many other young men her husband's grandfather who had been killed in the Great War. Her recently deceased husband had actually been born in my 17th century cottage which had belonged to his family for generations before him, and being in the area she had taken a chance of calling and asked if she and her grandchildren could have a look around. Readily consenting, over a cup of tea she hesitantly asked if I had ever experienced anything unusual in the house, there being one room upstairs where as a little boy her husband had been too afraid to enter. I immediately knew she meant the spare bedroom at the front of the cottage, which had an ancient diamond shaped pane window overlooking the rarely used lane which led down to the local train station. The first time my eldest daughter had stayed in that room, she awoke during the night to see a fair haired lady dressed in white move across the room and look out of that window. Assuming it was my wife in her nightdress she thought little of it until morning when she noticed my wife was wearing navy blue striped pyjamas. My wife and I had never seen my daughter's white lady, but both of us had often seen a complete void in the same corner of the room, which my wife thought of as a gateway. Showing the very spot to my visitor, she informed me it was her husband's great grandmother who had sat there every day even long after the war was over, watching for her eldest son to come up the lane on his return from the trenches, but who like Rudyard Kipling's own son sadly never came home. She later kindly sent me copies of some old family photographs taken in what was now my garden. As we paged through them to see how much the garden had changed over the decades, my daughter recognised her white lady straight away.

At poppy time last year I was on the train sitting opposite my Tunbridge Wells based work colleague and noticed his flower lacked the green paper leaf that comes as standard issue.

'You've been short-changed' I had said, 'you're missing a leaf and your poppy looks a bit worse for wear.'

As I stared and pointed at my friend's poppy his evasive behaviour and awkward guilty look struck me as suspicious. I took a closer look and lo and behold his poppy's central black button sported the legend 'Haig Fund', two little words that had been universally changed to 'Poppy Appeal' some ten years previous. I suspect my scrooge-like friend probably has a little tin at home containing all the commonly seen charity pins and flags labelled with the appropriate date for them to be worn 'lest he forget', and those he most likely bought with foreign coins!

I am rather more than tipsy as had been anticipated when I set off this morning, hence I wasn't allowed to take a book with me to study for fear of losing it along with my sensibility. Instead, there being little else to focus my attention on except the list of attendees in my souvenir booklet, I stare abstractedly at my reflection in the carriage window which I think looks very smart and officer-like wearing a dark suit, white shirt, regimental tie and rose. The number of Generals, Brigadiers, Colonels and other senior officers listed in my booklet confirms just how well St. George is supported by the military on this most drunken of days.

My own military experience although but a faint shadow of theirs, does nevertheless involve a considerable amount of drink...

THE COLONEL

My brother and I had been locked inside the quartermaster's store not as prisoners, but in sheer frustration by the sergeant in charge who told us he could take no more.

'You have ten minutes to help your bloody selves to anything you bloody well want!' He had shouted at us. 'When I come back from my tea break and let you out, I never want to bloody well see either of you here ever bloody again!'

That was our fourth Tuesday evening at the Territorial Army centre. Having joined the previous month, the deal was that you had to attend evening parade once a week, complete at least ten weekend exercises per year and participate at the Regiment's annual camp. In return you got to play at being soldiers, received a much needed by me weekly payment and tax free annual bonus, and were allocated a full set of uniform and accompanying kit. It was the latter items that had caused the sergeant to break with regulation and give us free rein in his otherwise hallowed store-room.

When you were initially issued with your uniform on joining the Regiment, the quartermaster sergeant and his assistant threw at you whatever looked like it might fit, and gave you ten minutes to try it on or change it if really necessary. After this he would only entertain swapping any items in exceptional circumstances and made sure we knew this really meant 'never'. He hadn't expected to come across two brothers who would spend hours parading back and forth at home in front of family, friends and mirrors, evaluating each item in turn.

The first week following our initiation we were both to be found waiting outside the store-room door. I had a couple of items of uniform I was still unhappy with, but Paul had brought the whole lot back for exchange. The second week I was queuing because we had had our helicopter experience and my poncho had proved to be leaky, but to the horror of the sergeant, Paul was simply unhappy because he had seen someone else with a nicer looking and better quality camouflage jacket and wouldn't go on another weekend away unless he could have the same. I thought the sergeant was going to hit him. Week three was even worse. The nicer and better quality camouflage jacket the sergeant had violently thrown at my brother the week before turned out to have stitch marks where someone else had previously sewn on and removed a badge and a corporal stripe.

'But you will get your own bloody badges and probably be a corporal yourself eventually, God forbid,' said the sergeant, 'then you can cover the stitch marks up. What do you think this is anyway; it's not bloody Harrods!'

'But I might not,' said Paul, 'and whenever I wear it, all I will keep thinking about is the unsightly stitch marks, and I won't be able to concentrate or shoot properly or anything.'

When he saw us waiting outside his door for the fourth time the sergeant was remarkably calm and seemed in a resigned mood, resting back against the doorframe, sighing and shaking his head from side to side.

'And what small fashion hiccup troubles you two dear sisters this time,' he asked.

'It's my mess tin', answered Paul, offering out the item before him with both hands as if he was Oliver Twist. 'I know I can't expect to have a brand new one and I can just about cope with the scratches on it, but someone has obviously burnt some milk or something in this one and the brown stain won't scrub out; my wife's tried everything.'

'It's a bloody mess tin!' screamed the sergeant. 'You are going to use it in the field and it is going to get massively scratched and burnt and far, far worse, and...' And so he had locked us inside.

I had found out about the Territorial Army from a work colleague who had been an Army helicopter pilot before changing career to be in insurance, but kept his hand in by becoming a member of the City based Honourable Artillery Company, a sort of specialist TA mainly for ex-officers. It only took one visit to my local TA centre to convince me that not only would I thoroughly enjoy getting involved, the extra pay would make a huge difference to my stretched income with having a young family to support. I only had to tell my brother I had taken the oath and become a soldier before he too signed up, desperate not to be left out. It was without doubt the best thing we had ever done together.

'C' Company, of the Queens 6/7th Infantry Regiment had its base near Gatwick Airport in a drill hall next to the local police station. The major advantage to this was that the police would join us after parade in the Naafi bar, which stayed open for as long as someone was still capable of drinking, and they made it plain that as long as you were wearing your beret, they wouldn't stop and breathalyse you on your drive home.

Paul and I immediately fitted in well with 'C' Company, partly due to our being brothers and thereby a bit of a novelty; partly due to us being older than the other new recruits; partly due to it being known we worked in the City and were therefore classed as 'toffs' by the officers; but mostly thanks to my brother's business expense account and his largesse at the bar. We were always first and last to order a round of drinks for all present. It also helped win the admiration of some of the harder cases amongst the rank and file, that I had let it be 'secretly' known we were planning a major armed robbery in the City and only operating under cover as businessmen, and that we had joined the TA to get access to weapons and to recruit key individuals. This admission followed an episode in the bar at our first shooting weekend, when a particularly hard case had held a knife to my stomach and asked why he shouldn't just slit me open, and I had to make something up on the fly. Shooting weekends were spent on the firing ranges usually somewhere on the coast, and involved drinking as much as possible on the Friday evening, then spending Saturday firing copious quantities of noisy live ammunition from rifles and machine guns, which was all very well if you weren't dehydrated and suffering a thumping headache from the night before.

Having access to cash and an air of mystery about us was important to Paul and I, having been singled out as potential officers from early on. As such we were very much in the no man's land of not being private soldiers and so different from the other men, but we still had a very long way to go to be in the officer corps and so didn't fit in there either. It also didn't help that most other potential officers we met were arrogant types more suited to Kitchener's nineteenth century army, and that we had to wear white flashes on our shoulders making us stand out as obvious targets for abuse.

It was the Regimental Colonel himself who had selected us for this accolade and alcohol may have had a role. As part of the recruitment process, we had to attend a selection weekend involving a lengthy session in the gym doing P.E.; followed by a practical lesson in hand to hand combat; then a three mile cross-country run in double quick time; a 'Dad's Army' style intelligence test using poles, wire and barrels taking it in turns to get your 'men' over an imaginary obstacle; and finally an assault course. It says much for how keen Paul was that he undertook all this activity having hurt his self in the gym exercise, but not realising until hours later in Accident and Emergency that he had actually broken a rib. A whole crowd of us new recruits had been bussed to the test centre on the Friday evening and all this fun was due to start at dawn on the Saturday morning, hence we were advised to climb into our sleeping bags early and get a good night's rest. Naturally Paul and I decided to go to a pub instead and returned very drunk and out of pocket after closing time, to find all the other babes-in-arms blissfully asleep but the Naafi bar still open. The only occupants were the barman, the Regimental Sergeant Major and the Colonel of the Regiment. Trying and failing to purchase a drink with the few pence we had left the Colonel summoned us over and bought us both a drink on his tab.

A few more pints of cider later we were still chatting amicably to this reputably unapproachable pair, and before I fell off my seat and was rightly sent to bed, Paul heard me ask the same personal questions over and over in a drunken and confused loop, possibly on the basis of some nagging I myself had received at home:

'So Colonel, what does your wife think of you spending all your time getting drunk with the TA?'

'So Colonel, what does your wife's wife think of you spending all your time getting drunk with the Sarnt-Major?'

'So Colonel, what does your wife's wife think of you spending all your time getting drunk with the Sarnt-Major's wife?'

I also made the fatal error when the barman dared to call final orders and the RSM ordered himself two more pints of beer, of pointing out that he already had four full pints hidden under his chair. I think the Colonel made us potential officers as a punishment and by way of revenge. The RSM certainly took **his** revenge the following day. Paul and I were ahead of the field in the three mile run and nearing the finish when from nowhere the RSM steamed up behind me and pushed me sideways into an eight foot deep ditch full of farm slurry.

Annual camp for the Regiment that year was based at Sennybridge training centre in Wales. The Brecon Beacons is a famous military training ground with what the Ministry of Defence describes as

163

'unforgiving terrain'. We certainly found the Welsh population fairly unforgiving especially in the *Usk and Railway* local village inn next to the camp. Here, despite there being three old ladies in large white lace aprons serving behind the bar and a motley collection of 'only Welsh spoken here' drinkers glaring moodily at us, we English couldn't expect to get served until someone called old Ted came along - and he never did. Instead, on one of our few free afternoons Paul and I decided to walk the seven miles to try and find somewhere more sociable in Brecon town centre.

I am not sure if it's because I am an Englishman or just my own bad luck, but I have never seen much of the 'welcome in the valleys' that the beautiful country of Wales is famous for. The last time I was there I had in the car my wife, eldest daughter and my Mother, and although I had a rough itinerary mapped out based around visiting the many and wonderful heritage steam railways, we hadn't organised anywhere to stay. On the first evening it was getting late and in desperation I pulled up outside a small bed and breakfast establishment advertising a vacancy, and negotiated what seemed a fair fee with the reluctant to speak English owner who was wearing carpet slippers, a filthy string vest attempting to hold in his huge beer belly, holding back a vicious and smelly Alsatian, and who wouldn't let me in until we had concluded our deal. Thankfully I hadn't paid in advance and the rooms were situated on the ground floor, for when we saw the

reeking room where the dog obviously spent most of its
time, with a colour scheme which looked like a party of
drunken decorators had dispensed with brushes and
instead projectile vomited the paint everywhere, we
climbed out of the window, Mother included, and sped
off in search of an hotel run by an English chain.

My brother and I hadn't walked far when an old WW2 Army ambulance pulled to a halt next to us, and a very violent looking skinhead sitting next to a one-armed corporal who was somehow managing to drive the vehicle, ordered us in no uncertain terms to get in the back. As I opened the door I saw the ambulance was packed with more skinheads from rival 'B' Company, and with our giveaway shoulder flashes looming large I resigned myself to losing a few more teeth and gaining a black eye or two. Our reputation had gone before us however, and the cream of the 'B' Company thugs merely wanted to show off how disciplined they could be, and were auditioning themselves to be involved in our bank heist. I suddenly twigged as to why Paul and I had been left undisturbed two nights before, when our 'C' Company barracks hut had been invaded by a gang from 'B' Company wielding pick-axe handles.

As we approached Brecon we were told to wait in the back of the vehicle until summoned. Next thing the ambulance screeched to an untidy halt in front of the statue of one of Britain's most famous soldiers, the Irishman Arthur Wellesley, situated in the centre of Brecon town square. Immediately the rear doors of the ambulance flew open and 'B' Company acting as if they were armed, burst forth from the back and surrounded the vehicle forming a very effective 'all round defence', knocking the startled populace sideways and bringing the local traffic to a standstill. The corporal now stepped round to the back of the ambulance, smartly saluted us with his only arm, and loudly announcing that 'Brecon had been secured', begged us to vacate the vehicle and enjoy our sojourn in the town. We were most impressed and even the Iron Duke might have grinned if he were not made of bronze, so a few bottles of rosé later, we joined them in the local hotel to buy them a round of drinks, and watch them torture with lighted matches some local Welsh lads who had been stupid enough to poke fun at the one-armed corporal.

There were a few skinheads in 'C' Company, but most of the men (there were also two women) turned out to ex full time soldiers who wanted to retain the camaraderie, and these included British army; foreign legionnaires; some special forces; at least one mercenary who had seen a lot of action in Rhodesia and enjoyed exchanging Africa stories with me; a psychopath; and one sergeant who always looked immaculate and imagined he was General George Patton with a similar lust for glory.

Our first field exercise away from the training centre was a struggle; not because the marching up and down mountainous terrain in full kit and carrying over twenty kilograms of equipment was arduous, although it was, but because we were given contradictory instructions as to how to behave. Our very stern instructor corporal was adamant we should behave as a modern unit, blending into the countryside by covering ourselves in mud, branches, bracken, blackening our faces and creeping through the undergrowth panther style, but General Patton was more concerned that we march in a neat and orderly fashion Second World War style with him swaggering out in front looking glorious. These two opposite paths were bound to collide and we ended up covered in the corporal's grime and hence being plagued by gnats, and the good sergeant had to be satisfied with sitting in a Land Rover posing into the rear view mirror, or throwing thunder-flashes at us when we least expected it, and dispensing soft drinks at hugely inflated prices when our limited water ration ran dry.

Tagging along with Paul and I was another potential officer by the name of Johns. Johns was a couple of years younger than me and didn't want to be an officer; he wanted to be a batman, our batman. From the outset this strange ginger haired individual had latched on to us by taking the adjoining bed in the barrack room and insisting on being in charge of our kit for us.

'Now you two run along to the Naafi and have a good drink,' he had said the first evening in a motherly fashion, 'I will put everything away neatly and organised, iron all your uniforms and make sure your boots have a regulation shine. I've always wanted to be an officer's batman and now I have two to look after, you can see I'm fully prepared.' And he proudly presented a home-made camouflage pattern housewife bag with his initials on it, full of assorted items including polishes, cloths, toothbrushes 'for the use of' and his trusty camouflage painted travel iron. What were we to say?

Now it was time to put up our small two-man tents for the evening and Johns was to share with me. It had been an exhausting day running around in the heat and avoiding being caught by 'B' Company who were acting as the enemy, and apart from those on guard duty we all climbed inside our sleeping bags just after dusk. Johns had in his housewife bag a camouflage painted alarm clock which was to wake us at 4.30 a.m., early enough to be on the march by first light.

When the alarm awoke me from a deep and refreshing sleep, I stuck my head through the ground-level tent flap to espy in the faint morning light twenty pairs of boots standing in a smart line. As I slowly raised my eyes upwards, I could see wearing these boots twenty grinning soldiers all fully dressed and with all their equipment packed and ready to go, and next to them a smirking sergeant trying to stifle a giggle, and a very, very angry corporal with ferocious eyes boring into mine.

As later related to me, what they all saw appear through the gloom when they came to attention in file that morning, was a lone tent still standing; then they heard an alarm clock going off half an hour late; then they saw a sleepy head appear through the flap and disappear back inside again; then they heard someone shout 'you bloody idiot!' and something metallic being broken; then they saw the tent start to rock and finally come collapsing down in a rope and canvas tangled confusion as a major fight ensued within. If it hadn't caused so much hilarity that even the corporal laughed Johns and I would have been in serious trouble.

Half way through week two, Johns, Paul and I were bundled into a lorry and driven to Aldershot where over two days we were to compete against a further twelve potential officers from various regiments for just six actual places on the course. This was a surprise to us and to General Patton who accompanied us for moral support, but three days later we arrived back at Sennybridge complete physical and emotional wrecks but all three of us successful. Apart from lots of running around, marching and many but far more complex 'Dad's Army' style tests of initiative, two things about this competition stand out. Firstly we had to each individually complete a challenging assault course whilst being observed and timed by a party of officers. Each obstacle on the course was painted in red and green with it being forbidden to touch the red areas. Putting everything into getting across or through these obstacles only to keep hearing 'wrong, do it again' was soul destroying. Secondly as a test of our presentation skills and ability to cope under pressure, we were given only ten minutes to prepare a five minute lecture on any subject, to be delivered to a panel of very important looking Colonels and Brigadiers. Of the three of us Paul went first and eulogised about the history and mysteries of the Lloyd's of London insurance market. What the panel particularly enjoyed was his opening line of:

'Traditionally, the eldest son of the gentry would inherit the family Estate, the second son would go into the Church, and the third son into the Army, but if he was too stupid and even the Army wouldn't take him, he'd go into Lloyd's.' Loud guffaws from the audience. (Actually I don't think much has changed.)

I followed and started by drawing a rough map of Africa on the blackboard in the room, placing a big heart shape where Malawi is to be found, and then describing my experience of unexpectedly coming across the Chinese Army covertly guarding any mining areas and other assets of importance. One Brigadier was sufficiently interested in my presentation that he asked me to submit a written report to his intelligence people, which I eventually did.

It now appears that China has one way or another bought and taken control of most of Africa's natural resources and as I write has just landed a rover on the Moon, no doubt with a view to eventually controlling that source of minerals as well.

Johns came last and very worryingly for Paul and I, this dark horse had decided to surprise us by revealing a lifelong fascination with being able to kill people without making a sound, and his having built up a vast library of books and curiosities relating to assassins and their craft. To support his lecture he held out various bottles of readily available chemicals that

170

when mixed became fatally poisonous, together with cheese wire and other sharp household instruments of instant silent death. When he had finished he put all this material back where he had taken it from – a home-made camouflage pattern housewife bag with his initials on it. Don't Panic! Don't Panic!

On the final afternoon of camp, Patton introduced Paul and I to a spa and steam room he had discovered incongruously situated beneath the village library, and we three were lounging in the hot whirlpool when Johns popped his head round the door to say that as the Page brothers hadn't been in camp to protest otherwise, we'd been volunteered for evening guard duty and needed to hurry back. This heralded a miserable end to our otherwise wonderful two week experience. But on reporting to the guard house and lining up with four other unfortunates, who should we find had been put in charge of the guard than our one armed corporal who for the first time we noticed had very close together eyes and a maniac look about him.

'In civvy street I am a road-sweeper' said he in a cold and measured tone as if daring us to make remark; and pacing back and forth as we stood rigidly to attention face front avoiding his eyes. 'I manage my cart with my one arm and the most people think of me is to spit on the pavement in front of me, sneer as they throw rubbish down for me to pick up, or point and laugh as I sweep up piles of dog-shit. In the army however,' getting louder and beginning to shake, 'I am a corporal and that means I am in charge. The rules of this camp state that after 10.00 p.m. everyone should be in their barrack huts with lights out, and in total silence. Up until now I have not observed those rules to have been enforced or obeyed. Tonight I am in authority and things will be different. You will each take with you a pick axe handle. If you see anyone regardless of rank, misbehaving, drunk, fighting or daring to disobey the curfew rules after 10.00 p.m. you will blow your whistle to call me and your fellow guard, you will then break either the culprit's collar bone thus' giving the soldier next to me a mighty thwak, 'or the shinbone thus' felling the poor man completely. So off we went on patrol and in minutes word had got around that this was the guard duty to volunteer for if you wanted a licence to be violent, and it ended up with as many people on patrol looking for trouble as were going about their innocent business. Paul and I just went and stood outside the window of the Naafi with Johns passing cider out to us, and got drunk, because we could, because we were the guard.

The company that supplied my brother with an expense account was a small but wealthy specialist marine insurance broker called Toomey & Co. Mr. Toomey was rarely to be seen although his eighteen year old son worked in the same office as Paul but would never have dared reveal what antics went on for fear of us telling his father he was a pervert. He was never really happy unless tied up semi-naked and having staples fired into him or needles thrust into him by the pretty young secretary, which was a bit disconcerting for the handful of elderly clerks who had to do their job and act as if nothing untoward was happening.

Many an evening I would go round to Paul's office after work to travel home with him, only to find some of our soldier friends in attendance with vast quantities of wine and vodka being dispensed by the pretty young secretary. One of our favourite games was office rugby. This was played using ledgers each of which weighed the same as a full suitcase, used for recording insurance transactions (this was the pre-computer age). We would throw these giant books at each other with the recipient having to catch them rugby ball fashion, or risk either the ledger being severely damaged or themselves receiving a serious injury. Toomey Junior never played this game but would instead be gagged and tied to a chair in the centre of the room with the books just missing his head as they flew from one side to the other. On one occasion I was bored and whilst the others were playing, decided to make a large upright metal coat stand into something more interesting and entertaining. By bending the arms back into a 'v' shape and then tying on Toomey Junior's thick elastic braces, I was able to create a very effective and very powerful catapult. Initially employing paperclips as ammunition and firing the weapon within the office, I smashed the glass covering two expensive watercolours before being reprimanded and told to instead address targets in the street outside (I had also upset one of Paul's colleagues by firing a tin of coffee powder at him which had burst, covering his entire head which was already sweat soaked from playing rugby with a brown sticky goo and making him look like an Indian). The office was on the first floor of the building and overlooked a steady stream of commuters rushing through the rain on their way to London Bridge station. With the paperclips having little effect on such large mobile targets wearing raincoats and holding umbrellas, the ammunition increased in calibre to embrace staple guns, hole punches, ink pads and stamps, sticky tape dispensers and anything else of a heavy and dangerous nature. As only to be expected there was now a queue of people wanting to have a go; it became a competition, and a strict system of scoring was established for damage and/or injury caused. The transparent raindrops on the windows changing to reflect a flashing blue put paid to this little escapade.

Unfortunately, some of our military friends would get overexcited and exuberant when they joined us in the City, especially after a liquid afternoon. The problem was they were impressed with our knowledge of the City and wanted to demonstrate some of their own particular specialism. We were standing with General Patton in a very busy Leadenhall Market pub just after work one evening, when my brother recognised further down the bar the individual who had been instrumental in his being sacked from his previous job, and made the mistake of pointing him out.

'Finish your drinks gentlemen, exit the premises in a calm and measured manner and position yourselves discreetly across the road if you will,' said Patton.

We didn't have long to wait before Patton exited the pub from a side door and disappeared into the market. Nothing happened for a few long seconds and then pandemonium broke out as everyone else fought to exit the pub together, all choking and with eyes streaming. Patton had let off a CS gas canister.

Even more enthused than the glory seeking sergeant was an ex SAS character called Jim. He had introduced us to some friends of his (more ex SAS) who did specialist work for insurance companies providing kidnap and ransom protection. In the event of someone with appropriate cover being abducted, the ex SAS boys would endeavour to get them back so saving the insurers a hefty ransom bill. Jim and two of his friends were in Paul's office one evening and as usual there was a rumpus. Suddenly by way of complaint there was a rude knocking on the wall, coming from the office next door. This rarely used office was being temporarily occupied by one of Mr. Toomey's business friends and was accessed from our office via a corridor.

'We don't want our fun being spoilt, have a word with him would you Jim?', asked my brother, expecting Jim to walk round and merely look military and threatening to the spoilsport next door.

The next second there was an almighty crash as Jim literally walked through the wall, caving his way through the plasterboard and wooden battens using karate kicks and punches, and revealing a white powder covered elderly man on the other side, sitting at his desk amidst the debris and frozen in absolute shock and terror. The poor man never dared tell anyone what had happened, and we simply kept that office locked and bought a floor to ceiling map of Great Britain to tape to our side of the wall so covering up the person shaped hole.

We sadly never did get to finish our training and pass out as officers at Sandhurst as too many complications got in the way. For one thing, Paul had set up in business with the 'coffee headed' colleague; had become involved in a rather silly insurance transaction and lost his liberty; and our Dad who a couple of years previously had been embroiled in a rather more serious insurance scandal (albeit he was quite rightly never convicted of anything), had lost all his wealth along with his self esteem and had become ill to the extent he never would recover. Paul and I always felt and acted like officers however, and one evening many years later I even got to become one!

In 2005 I was invited to an informal cocktail party held by the Conservative City Circle, an august body with the aim of cultivating Tory support within the City, as if that was necessary. I had as usual had an interesting and rather too liquid lunch and so arrived very late bringing along my eldest daughter, then in her early twenties, both for her education and because I knew I would be bored stiff on my own.

Waiting patiently at the reception desk was a young lady (by her demeanour destined to be a high Tory one day); with in front of her one sticky-backed name badge, we being the last to arrive.

'Kirkman-Page' I announced, to which she responded with a beaming smile; leaping to her feet; thanking me over and over; sort of bowing and curtseying in a confused manner; slapping the sticky-backed name badge on my chest and running off whilst excitedly shouting:

'The Colonel's here, the Colonel's here.' And sure enough on closer inspection my badge did say Colonel Page.

Within seconds a man (apparently the Chairman of the City Circle) ran up to me, grabbed my hand and dragged me into a room of some two hundred suited guests and dignitaries, saying:

'Thank-you for coming Colonel, oh how wonderful, oh thank-you for your support, oh what joy', and similar pleasantries over and over whilst pumping my hand with his two hands and bowing down in a fawning sort of way.

'You simply must meet our key speaker Oliver Letwin', said the Chairman.

'Make way for the Colonel, make way for the Colonel!' he shouted as he thrust me through the milling throng towards his intended target, elbowing other guests forcibly aside.

'Make way, make way' he gasped, pulling me with him and pushing aside a crowd of sycophants gathered around the then shadow Chancellor of the Exchequer.

'I hope you will let me know what you think of my speech, Colonel' said Oliver once we had been introduced. Of course I would.

'Who else is here?' I asked the Chairman.

'Theresa May (then the Shadow Leader of the House of Commons and now in 2013 the incumbent Home Secretary), let me find her for you, oh do please wait here for me', and off he ran.

In the meantime feeling in need of refreshment I spotted and accosted a very tall, very black waiter who was passing by holding two bottles of champagne and some glasses.

'You are from central Africa' said I, taking a chance on the blackness of his skin pinpointing his likely origins, and he grinned broadly and told me in a deep majestic voice that I was indeed correct.

'I would like you to follow me with your two bottles and only serve my daughter and I unless I say otherwise' I instructed him, assuming an officer-like air of authority. And so when the Chairman returned to collect me there were now three in my party as we made our way across the room to meet our next celebrity.

'Make way, make way for the Colonel', happened all over again and all of a sudden we were in front of Miss May. At this stage some of the champagne and the lunchtime drinks were catching up with me, so I told Miss May in all honesty how far more pretty and feminine she looked in person having only seen her on

TV, how she looked the sort of girl I could have gone out with her being the same age as me, how Theresa was one of my favourite names, how she must have some champagne from my new black friend, and I put my protective arm round her and gave her a cuddle whilst introducing her to my more amused than astonished daughter.

After much more champagne and some boring speeches I again found myself face to face with Oliver Letwin who was keen on my feedback.

'You came across as Sergeant Wilson from Dad's Army' I said, 'you need to lose the namby-pamby voice and be far more positive if we are going to get those awful people out of government. If I was Tony Blair listening to that speech I would be clapping my hands with glee'. Things went downhill from there both for me **and** the Conservatives.

TRAIN No.10 ^CALLING_AT:^ Bermuda Shorts

I am back on my normal route into London and on the late morning train again. It is many months since I have seen them, but there is no mistaking the extremely large boy and his cow, who are obviously just as delighted to renew my acquaintance, because they make a point of sitting opposite me, crushing my legs into a corner, and spread an array of smelly food items before them on the table between us. The boy has grown much larger in the intervening period and is almost a match for his mother, making them look a little like Tweedledum and Tweedledee. He has also been promoted to the brass section of his band, and accordingly swapped the 'pop bottle' clarinet for a bassoon style version, from which he is suckling lustily. The cow meanwhile is having one of those loud one-sided conversations in her mobile phone, only she has the even more annoying habit of conversing in an '*I said – she said*' style.

With my shoulders beginning to hunch as I become increasingly frustrated, I am fast losing the battle to try reading about famous inventors, because before me is a text book focusing on the anthropogenic contribution to our planet, people such as Archimedes, Leonardo da Vinci, and even Jacques Cousteau of aqualung fame. I actually invented something once; a way of doing global business electronically before the

180

www was invented. I am even named on a patent, but sadly I wasn't far enough ahead of my time and the www **did** come along and spoilt everything.

A few years ago my eldest daughter bought me a wonderful invention, the TV-B-Gone. I had thrown away my own TV as part of creating an environment in which to study (although the BBC Licensing people fail to believe me and regularly correspond with me on the subject - it's a bit like having a pen friend although some of the letters are quite threatening), and once you learn to live without a TV and become completely out of touch with what is happening in that two-dimensional world, it is amazing how irritating it is having background TV invade your life when trying to converse in a bar, office or shop. Being able to discreetly press my TV-B-Gone button and zap whatever is showing gives me a great feeling of power. Even more rewarding is zapping the whole TV wall in an electrical appliance showroom just for the hell of it. What would be nice to have is a Mobile-B-Gone, maybe someone has already invented one. Even better would be an Oldgit-B-Gone. I for one would use my device to send a few volts through the old man sitting the other side of the aisle and who has annoyed me on far too many an occasion. He is the man whom most commuters will recognise as taking forever to sit down; farting around putting his things on the rack above; holding up all the other passengers who want to move down the train meanwhile; swishing his coat into your face as he disrobes, and then finally taking his seat, only to get up again at least twice more; first to get his newspaper out of his bag; and then if it has been raining, to move his wet umbrella along the rack so it drips water onto my head and not his. I would of course have already pressed the password protected 'use with caution' button and electrocuted the two 'Looking Glass' characters opposite me, who would now be nothing more than smouldering heaps of black ooze ruining the upholstery. But I am getting carried away and wandering into the realms of fantasy.

I did actually meet a couple of inventors. The first was the father of a quiet lad my age, who went to the same local youth club as me when we were sixteen. I remember one Christmas he asked if I would come to his father's Christian Bible Club evening with him, followed by door to door carol singing. As I was dressed in be-studded denim and biker leathers at the time (I only had a bright yellow moped, but pretended it was a real motorbike and that I was really tough), I thought him somewhat deranged. But when he informed me that he was fed up being the only male at the Bible Club, and that all the other thirty regular attendees were pretty girls, I even gave him a lift on the pillion!

I never did find out what his father invented, but that was his official job title – Inventor. He didn't look the part appearing far too normal and not wearing glasses, but he did have a nice posh house with solar panels, before people had solar panels; so unless it was inherited money, he was obviously successful.

The second inventor was a youngish man I had met through a business colleague, who lived in Bermuda, and who *was* from a wealthy family. Not having to try too hard at being successful therefore, and as a consequence not having been too successful, he had decided to reinvent himself as - an inventor. He had looked long and hard at all the fantastically expensive yachts and motor-launches in Bermudan harbours, and noticed that they all had costly security systems, burglar alarms, CCTV and the like. He had also thought long and hard about what would happen, if the threat to these vessels came not from the land or by boat, but from below. He envisaged armies of pirates and intruders arriving by mini-sub or using Monsieur Cousteau's aqualungs, and so decided to 'invent' underwater CCTV. To test his great idea, he started by making a large hole in the bottom of the hull of his father's huge and expensive yacht. When he later returned to fit the camera he had absentmindedly left on the quayside, the yacht was not quite the floating palace it had once been. Instead, it was sitting on the ocean floor, and quite ruined. When I saw him again a few months later his family were still refusing to talk to him, and he'd decided to become a famous golfer instead, having just had his first lesson.

BERMUDA SHORTS

My parents spent a great deal of my teenage years travelling on business, and one of their favourite destinations was Bermuda. I fell in love with the very idea of the island having listened to their stories, and with the romanticism of the famous Bermuda Triangle and its supposed portal to other Worlds, most especially with the disappearance of flight 19 which triggered the writing of many a spooky novel in the mid 1970's. I have since been to Bermuda numerous times, both on business and for pleasure.

Bermuda lies in the Atlantic Ocean, about 1,000 miles North-East of Miami, and is a fascinating island with a very distinctive and deliberate British feel to it. Unless you live in Bermuda you can't own or even hire a car, and so the best way to enjoy the sights, take in the wonderful scents, and listen to the endless but tuneful chatter of tropical birds and twilight driven tree frogs is by moped, and with virtually no traffic it is wonderful to putter along the twisting lanes of the island wearing nothing more than a pair of Bermuda shorts, sandals, and an obligatory ugly looking cork-lined and therefore utterly useless helmet with plastic side earpieces, dating from the 1960's.

Once a seventeenth century base for privateers seeking to plunder treasure from passing merchantmen and avoid the hated 'revenue', Bermuda is now a favourite for companies that have already amassed a lot of treasure but whose Director's also want to avoid paying anything to the hated 'revenue'. Seen therefore as an exclusive paradise for rich tax-exiles and offshore captive insurance companies, the population is sparse, and if you know where to go, anyone can enjoy an entire beach to themselves, the island boasting hundreds of exclusive and stunning coves. When I was first there I sat on just such a beach in splendid isolation and warm sunshine, with salmon pink coral sand between my toes; looking out at the turquoise sea with the stark white breakers crashing over the coral reef fringing the small bay; imagining the days of pirates and Robinson Crusoe, and thinking fond memories of my sadly departed Father. Dad once gave me a tie he had been given by the

185

owner of his favourite restaurant on the planet which happens to be in Bermuda, called the Lobster Pot. The tie was blue with red lobsters on it. I lost that original tie along the way of life but luckily managed to beg a replacement from the same restaurant when my current and forever wife and I enjoyed mouth-watering rum lashed lobster bisque there many years later. I can't wear that tie without a rush of exotic Bermudan tastes, smells and visions flooding my senses.

The last time I was on the island, I was with a client of mine. There was a definite business opportunity I had established through people I knew from previous visits, but my client, owning his own small and embryonic company was on a very limited expenses budget. So although he agreed to pay my airfare, we had agreed to share a room at a (relatively for such an expensive island) low cost, small, but nevertheless beautiful family run hotel. I have never minded sharing rooms with business partners to reduce cost, especially having owned and run my own company and being mind-full of cash-flow. The only problem I have is mine and that is that I snore not only for England but for the entire planet. My wife blames it on the amount I drink, and I would be inclined to agree but for the experience of my elder brother Paul who eventually went to stay at Her Majesty's pleasure in Ford open prison. He snored just as loudly as me; in fact we had the same sound and pitch of voice, for on the phone no-one could tell us apart which made for interesting conversations with wives and girlfriends. After a month in prison however and assumedly no alcohol, he was put in solitary confinement for his own good as the other inmates in his dormitory could take no more of the nightly decibel bombardment, and had threatened to summarily end his life in the toilet block.

Three particular self-related snoring occasions immediately spring to mind, my wife could mention many thousands of others. One was when I was on business in New York on behalf of my own software company, and booked in to a small hotel on Wall Street, sadly since destroyed by Al Qaeda. I arrived with a business colleague whom I had also agreed to share a room with to reduce cost. We were late arriving at the hotel it being near midnight by the time we reached the Wall Street area, but luckily our room had been held for us, and we were greeted by two giggling night desk porters, who were delighted to meet 'Julian and Jeremy' who would be sharing a room (hah hah, nudge nudge). It did not help that Jeremy, despite being a very serious business man, with his 'obviously dyed hair', and tendency to wear bright coloured blazers with dark trousers, always came across looking like a game show host.

Aware of my snoring issue (I have never considered it an actual problem it rarely having bothered me), I suggested that Jeremy should retire half an hour ahead of me and I would follow after a drink or two served in the lobby by the giggling twins. It was only when I finally entered our room I was reminded of the fact that Jeremy only had one leg. For here was his other leg proudly standing in the middle of the room between the single beds, wearing a sock and a shoe and balancing the same on top. I also noticed that he had brought a few strange keepsakes with him to make him feel at home such as family pictures, a strange box, and even a small vase; perhaps there was someone in it.

His being one legged also came into memorable use. That same trip we stopped off in Miami to attend one of those events that only American companies can host; a customer evening extravaganza, where hundreds of their customers pay large sums of money to be marketed at, to get paralytic, listen to has-been rock bands, and hear some words of wisdom from the company president the following morning. On this occasion we skipped the pre-lunch words of wisdom (we were recovering from getting paralytic, and too much dancing to the has-been bands), and decided to go swimming in the warm Atlantic off Ocean Boulevard. It being out of season the beach was fairly quiet, although along from us were what sounded and looked like a Galapagos party of sea-lions dressed as Americans, with the overly large women talking annoyingly loudly in a horribly grating 'twanging' accent. Jeremy and I entered the water, and swam up opposite these beached mammals near to where the shark nets cease. I heartily shouted 'shark' a few times, and we both thrashed about in the water to which the beach reacted by sitting up and staring open-mouthed at us. Having gained their full attention, I dragged a now screaming Jeremy and his wagging stump up the beach towards the now fleeing, waddling, squealing blubbery gathering. Had it been a real shark attack we were well and truly left to our own devices.

The second memorable snoring event was on a wonderful trip my eldest daughter Alexandra and I undertook to Guernsey on one of the BT Global Challenge yachts. It was only a weekend away, but I had bought it in a charity auction raising money for a friend of mine and unknowingly bidding against my wife who was hoping to buy the trip as a present for me; hence we paid three times the next lowest bid. No matter, it was a fantastic trip. You keep watches on a boat which means you take it in turns to manage the vessel whilst others get some sleep, and my daughter and I had bagged the middle of the night watch. This was together with Axel, a huge Norwegian who would take the helm, and Suicide Steve, so nicknamed by me because he was so manic depressive I tried to encourage him to disappear over the side during our watch, promising not to raise the alarm. That night my daughter and I sat huddled together at the prow of the yacht looking up at a Milky Way you only ever see from the ocean or in a desert, too mind-boggled by the number of stars and vastness of the firmament to speak; and when we glanced down at the sea the bioluminescence was an equal contender for first place in a catalogue of wonderment. At last however it was our turn to go to sleep and Axel approached me, tentatively explaining that as he and I were sharing a bunk bed in a tiny cabin, I should be alerted to the fact that he is a champion snorer, renowned throughout

Oslo. Having explained my own snoring capabilities with ample backup from my daughter, we agreed a competition was in order; that we would go to bed at the same time, and meet to decide a winner in the morning. The excitement of the day, the wonder of all that I had seen and experienced, and the fresh sea air turned me within seconds of climbing into my cot into that wonderful state of being, known as a log; something a Norwegian should be eminently at home with.

In the morning Alexandra and I were on deck enjoying a self-fried breakfast and drawing in the sounds, scents and rhythm of a yacht-based sunrise at sea, when Axel put in an appearance, shook my hand to congratulate me, and with tears running down his crestfallen face vanished downstairs not to be seen again until we made home port in Southampton.

On the third occasion, I had taken my wife and both teenage daughters on a camping weekend to beautiful Dorset in the south west of England (and mainly for me to secretly enact some scenes from my favourite comedy play 'Nuts in May' by Mike Leigh). I had selected a campsite similar to the one in the play, basically a field on a slope with few facilities. At the lower end of the field were already established a collection of large expensive looking family sized tents and caravans all huddled close to one-another, and strategically positioned around a community camp fire intended for use that evening. We had turned up in a posh convertible car, but we had only brought two cheap and nasty two-man tents and we pitched them at the top of the field, deliberately well away from the others. Within minutes our lower field neighbours had sent a delegation to find out who we were; invite us to tea; tell us our tents would be washed away should it rain as we had chosen bad ground; tell us that my tacky tent looked inside out; implore us to join in with the community singing to be held that evening; and basically interfere whilst having a good nose.

We ignored the friendly advice and the invitation to tea, and abandoned our tents to explore the surrounding Nuts in May highlights. These included the Jurassic coast delights of Lulworth Cove, Stair Hole and Corfe Castle, and for good measure, we completed our day out with a delightful steam train ride inclusive of a silver service evening dinner on the Swanage Railway which conveniently ran parallel to the campsite, and the friendly train driver even made a special stop to drop us off afterwards.

When we eventually returned to our tents, the campfire was blazing and the singing was in full voice with strains of the awful gibberish scouting song 'ging gang goolie', followed by the even more repulsive 'kum ba yah' floating up towards us. Two ghastly spotty boys even turned up to encourage us all (but especially my daughters) to join the fifty or so revellers below. By that stage I must have been overtired from all the driving (it couldn't possibly have been the many bottles of wine and cider I had consumed) and I decided to stagger straight to the tent. Within seconds (my wife tells me) an *enormously deep sonorous snoring burst forth from within the canvas, so loud that the singing came to an abrupt halt and all eyes were focused up the hill. My daughters giggled thinking I was just playing the fool but my wife knew better; the noise thundered on and on interspersed with animal grunting sounds, and it became clear that nothing would outperform the din until the dawn chorus finally took over. As my wife and daughters embarrassingly snuck away to hide inside their sleeping bags, they realised the revellers had also given up trying to compete and their evening had been brought to a premature close.*

Consequently, on the first night in the small but nevertheless beautiful hotel in Bermuda, I had said to my small but certainly not beautiful client friend:

'Please go to bed at least an hour in advance of me as I snore very, very loudly'.

'No' said he confidently, 'I have always slept soundly and nothing can keep me awake when I have a mind to it!' He was not a tall man and had a tendency to stamp and gesticulate with his arms to emphasise points, which when these points were quite minor seemed rather unnecessary but interesting to behold. So be it!

At some stage during that night he had, perhaps in the manner of some evangelistic preacher, 'gathered together' every spare pillow and cushion in the room he could find, coupled with two spare duvets lurking in the back of a wardrobe; piled the entire mass on my head, and jumped up and down on the resultant mound he had created. All this was with a view to silencing me perhaps forever, but all to no effect. I awoke to an angry, tired, miserable wretch of a client sitting on the end of his bed, glaring at me through eyes the pits of which would have led me to an everlasting flame-based torment. Having had a wonderful night's sleep myself, totally unaware of his nocturnal activities, and somewhat confused as to where all the bedding had come from.

The following evening was the occasion of my greatly upsetting the son of the lady who owned the hotel, none other than the celebrated, but much shorter than I would have imagined, and very scruffily dressed Michael Douglas. I have already mentioned it was but a small hotel. The hotel bar was very welcoming, held perhaps fifteen people at a push, but only had a very limited number of high stools to sit on, which were strategically placed around the room and all taken. My client and I were standing against one wall, not wanting to take up any of the limited, strategically placed high stools, and talking to a charming elderly couple from New York. We were shortly joined by the hotel's one honeymoon couple who were tired from having been walking around the island, she being too timid to risk the moped ride (or perhaps too fashion sensible to want to wear the awful 60's helmet).

'You must have a stool' said I to the new bride in gallant mood ably and copiously assisted by my invisible friend Monsieur Sauvignon Blanc whom I had been in active discussion with for a couple of bottles or so. Upon scanning the room however, I could only espy one stool vacant of bottom. This was the stool not being sat upon, but instead being utilised as a kind of lectern by the scruffy Michael Douglas, whom by now I had recognised as an actor of sorts, and who was playing court to an awful ensemble of giggling, loud, fawning, bobbing, dandyish sycophants. Every time King Michael spoke they would collectively bow low and fawn, simper or titter as if part of some woollen flock.

'Have you seen my latest reviews?' he might have asked - fawn and simper.

'Have you noticed I have a new photograph of myself I dish out to my adoring fans?' he might have asked – fawn, simper and titter.

'Did you know I inherited this large hole in my chin from my father?' he might have asked - fawn, simper and titter and an adventurous giggle from one of the more nonchalant acolytes.

'Are you using this stool?' I did ask, having crossed the room and addressing the King himself.

No fawning, no simpering, no tittering this time – just a sharp intake of many breaths! I was not only unanswered, I was completely ignored. A royal head was tossed, and a royal back was turned on me, but the stool was left momentarily unhanded. I swiftly stole the stool and carried it back triumphantly to the honeymoon bride. The room became deathly silent; the honeymoon lady turned ashen; all eyes were upon me, and I turned round to see the Douglas kingdom collectively staring at me in shock; King Michael himself was wearing a truly horrid, evil face; pointing at me and shaking in anger. But worse was to come. Within seconds his Queen arrived, the lovely Catherine Zeta-Jones. Having made her grand entrance to much acclaim from the sycophantic entourage (one of whom may even have feigned to majestically sweep the carpet before her), this was followed almost immediately by much whispering, and moments later by her following the King's pointed finger aimed at the awful, awful man who dared to steal her husband's throne. Luckily, Monsieur Sauvignon regularly tells me to see the funny side of things and so I started laughing in a buffoon like manner, prodding the stolen stool, rocking it too and fro, pointing back and leering at them, all of which responses seemed to make the indignation of the Douglas kingdom far worse.

Finally, and much later, most people had been in for dinner and it was bedtime. I had been banished to the bar for an hour by my client, who had learnt his lesson and had stamped off to our room to try and achieve some sleep in advance of my attempting base camp of mount pillow. The hotel was silent except for me and the barman chatting together amicably, and then the King and Queen came in for a nightcap. The barman naturally had to ignore me to serve them, and then he was told in no uncertain terms to ignore me anyway. The King and Queen then made a deliberate show of ignoring me themselves by talking loudly over and around me as if I was not only beneath their contempt, but completely invisible. And so we all had a great time enjoying ignoring each other (especially me who mentally auditioned for the role of being invisible by staring straight ahead and not moving, and then switching their drinks glasses when they weren't looking), and all because I upset his kingdom for the sake of a stool. No wonder I have never seen Michael Douglas play Henry the Fifth!

```
┌─────────────────────────────────────────────┐
│                    CALLING                    │
│  TRAIN No.11        AT:    The Mallard        │
│                                               │
└─────────────────────────────────────────────┘
```

Yet more months have gone by, I am into year three of my degree, and I have become a regular traveller on the Hastings to London line. I suppose I could now class myself as a **proper** commuter, in as much as I catch the same train every day (the 06.32); I always sit in the same carriage and at the same table with four seats; I sit with the exact same people who I have become quite comfortable with; and I generally respect the unwritten carriage rules. These naturally include: don't make any noise; don't make any fuss; don't make any mess; don't look at anyone. In fact at this unearthly hour the carriage is a bit like a morgue, with everyone except me sleeping soundly (and I should know because I sometimes stay with a friend who has a flat on the same floor as a funeral parlour, and I always wake up smelling strongly of formaldehyde). There is a strange soporific quietude throughout the journey as well, only enhanced by the soft but regular drumming of the wheels on the tracks, and the even softer but as regular nodding of eighty sleepy heads. Even the carriage lights seem to be subdued and dimmer than usual, as if they too know this is a time for solemnity. In fact some of my fellow travellers could actually be dead it is so tranquil. In Victorian times, some paranoid people used to have a little bell fitted to the outside of their 'safety coffin', which they could ring if they had been assumed dead from cholera, but were actually in a coma and suddenly came 'alive'. Perhaps the train company should provide 'safety hats' adorned with a little bell, for these early morning commuters to wear.

After many weeks of travelling together, the three businessmen sharing my table know my name, and are aware of the fact I am a mature student. Other than that, we are ignorant of each other, and would be horrified if any one of us tried to be more sociable, or to strike up a conversation of any meaningful kind – another unwritten rule. The latest hand the Open University have dealt me is to study the geological history of the British Isles. This may sound quite straightforward, but it actually involves reading a book in which every other paragraph refers to a set of co-ordinates on a vast map accompanying the course. The only way I can progress therefore, is to get my three table companions, to each tuck a corner of the map under their chin before they nod off, so becoming a huge human chart table for me to work from. This causes much amusement for the elderly ticket inspector who dutifully makes his rounds half way through the journey, but is always too timid to dare wake anyone up. Perhaps he also thinks some of his passengers might have passed away and is too squeamish to touch them lest they be stone cold. The current paragraph points me in the direction of the man opposite's midriff, Leicestershire. This is a county famous for many things of a geologic nature, but especially for its favourite son, Daniel

Lambert; at one time reputed to be the World's heaviest man, weighing in at 50 stones; which puts him in the 'overwhelmingly large', soft-bodied blob category. I remember as a child seeing a pair of his trousers at Leicester museum, which could easily fit a grown man in each leg, but which these days might simply be classed as XXXL. Daniel died 200 years ago, but the oldest rocks in this region are around 500 million years of age, and they contain important fossils of soft-bodied blobby jellyfish and worm-like creatures. It would be too far-fetched to suggest Mr. Lambert was in any way directly connected to this fossil world; but my Mother was from Leicester and in her old photo albums I now treasure, one of her beau's before she met my Dad, does look a little worm-like beneath his gay and frivolous exterior. They were on stage together in Gilbert and Sullivan's *HMS Pinafore*. Mum played the role of Buttercup and the worm played the boatswain.

I am glad Dad came along and took her away from Leicester. I was last in Leicester a few years ago, but that was to take her back there again…

THE MALLARD

It was 2006 and there were just a handful of us making our way on foot, down to where my Mum used to play as a child, and where we knew she would be happiest. In our party there was Mum's twin sister Lillian and her husband Mighty Mervin – both in their eighties; my two daughters Alex and Tiff - both in their early twenties; my brother Paul; and my wife Lolly and I. Oh, and Mum was in the bronze coloured plastic urn inside the supermarket carrier bag I was holding.

Lillian had chosen the spot to scatter Mum's ashes having known her forever of course; and because we had her twin with us, it was almost as if Mum was there in spirit as well as in pellets. In fact after the funeral a few short weeks before, we had made the wake an outrageous party in the restaurant opposite Mum's flat, with my brother and I insisting that all the mourners wear silly hats; and behaving in just the same maniac way we had so often done when she was alive. Mum would have had a typically fantastic time, and in spirit she no doubt did.

Mum, or Nana, or Margaret, or 'Greta' as they say up North, was born and brought up in Leicester. The house they lived in backed onto the Midland Mainline railway which ran along a deep cutting at the bottom of their garden. The cutting featured the odd tunnel and was traversed by countless bridges, one of which we now crossed to lead down to the Leicester tributary of the Grand Union canal. The railway has long gone and the cutting has been filled in, but the bridge work is still there and my youngest daughter Tiffany was keen to walk across the brickwork, all of four feet above the road surface.

'Greta used to walk across that same bridgework when she was about five years old' said Lillian, 'but then it was at least a fifty foot drop to the tracks below, and she used to lean over to see down the funnels of the engines as they roared past on their way to London. Her dress would whip around in the wind from the train and we never knew if she would be thrown backwards onto the road or sucked down onto the carriage roofs and killed. She was fearless!'

What Lillian didn't know was that when Paul and I were little kids on our annual visit to see Nana and Grandpa at Leicester, when the whole adult family were sitting in a far too small and hot front room, chatting in that Nancy Leicestershire 'I'll go to the foot of our stairs' accent over tea and cake; pretending they were pleased to see each other; not jealous of what each family had achieved in the past year; and competing in how well their children were becoming models of society; we, together with Lillian's eldest boy Nigel (who looked a bit like a young Oliver Reed) would also be out playing on those bridges. More than that, we would play on the tracks themselves taking it in turns to be the last to jump clear as a train came hurtling by. Most times, and given sufficient duration between trains, we would pile objects on the track to hopefully create a derailment as in the war movies so in vogue at the time. Luckily, being so young and small we were never able to build anything of consequence to a 100 ton engine steaming along at 100 mph. If it was a slow goods train however, the driver would often stop and the fireman and guard would chase us up the bank ready to give us a good hiding or worse, but we were never caught - even at five years old fear lent wings to my legs. I even remember hiding with the other boys in a tunnel waiting for a train to come through. They have small recesses in tunnels for workers to hide in if they are caught unawares. It was in one of these we were first hiding when Nigel warned us that the suction from the engine as it passed would pull us under the wheels. So we were all screaming, Nigel included, as the tunnel went black, the roaring locomotive approached, and the screeching of the steel wheels on steel track, the heat, the boiling water and the imagined pull of the train towards imminent death, terrified us all to the point of ecstasy. I had never been so excited in my young life.

Before our walk, we had actually stopped at the old house where the family used to live, and knocked on the door to ask if we could see the garden. As with most of Leicester, the house was now owned by an Asian family who kindly let us look around and even offered us lunch when they learnt that Lillian had been born there. Lillian pointed out where the old sheds had been, her dad's workshop, and the railings where she and we had stood and looked down on the trains below, before climbing down the bank to the track when the adults went inside. She also showed the new owner where the WW2 Anderson air-raid shelter was buried; and sure enough when he quickly dug with a spade the steps down to the shelter came to light, to much excitement and a promise that he would excavate the entire thing for prosperity.

Next door used to live a train driver, and sure enough the curious neighbour peering over the fence turned out to be none other than the son of said driver. I remembered his father because he was a driver of the famous 'Master Cutler' express train from London to Sheffield which went past the house at a million miles an hour. To my young imagination he was the driver of the fastest steam train ever called the 'Mallard', and as a treat at Christmas he would take us down to the huge engine sheds by the canal. We had to get up before dawn for this treat. The stone hot water bottles Nana always put in our beds were still warm from the night before and we would pull on as many layers of clothes as we could find before meeting up at the front of the house as planned. There, our magical driver would lead us in a little train of boys like the pied piper, following his oil lamp down to the engine sheds where at that time of the morning, monsters lived.

There would be at least twenty locomotives being got into steam for the day ahead; black leviathans with red fiery bellies, gushing smoke from their funnels and steam from their shiny wheels and pistons. We had to be careful how we crossed the tracks, quite steep for small feet and little legs and thick with oil, tar, coal, and black ooze. Despite the cold and the wind blowing sleet into your face, the occasional waft of heat from an engine would warm you to the marrow and send a thrilling shiver through your small frame. The noise was all around and the fantastic never to be forgotten smells all pervading. Once I remember being right by the side of a track and seeing a ghostly mist approach soundlessly towards me, only to become a small shunter engine pulling some coal trucks, towering monstrously over me but too slow and too quiet to make an impression against the wider cacophony of its larger sister engines. It was like something out of a fairytale.

Then our magical driver would lift us into the cab of his enormous black locomotive where the fireman would already be undressed to his shirt and sweating profusely as he shovelled endless amounts of coal from the tender into the gaping jaws of the giant furnace. Then the shovelling would stop, we would all crouch down and the fireman would put his shovel upside down into the fire to heat it up so it glowed a deep winter sunset red. Then on the back of the black shovel he would put on some streaky bacon and crack open some eggs, and within seconds we would tuck into the most fantastic breakfast imaginable; sitting inside a warm and cosy engine cab; knowing we shouldn't by rights be there and knowing we had to hide in the tender if the driver's boss (the Fat Controller) should come along (he never did); looking out at the Sun coming slowly up over a snowy winter horizon; listening to the engine come alive as the brass gauges moved towards full steam; smelling that wonderful hot breakfast smell coupled with all the engine smells and the cold piercing winter air; being with your little pals on a Christmas morn; massive ear to ear smiles on our faces dimpling our cheeks; and looking back at it, because we were such little boys - without a single care in the World. And on top of all that, when we got home the family would only just be stirring, we had already had the most fantastic adventure imaginable, and it was Christmas!

We passed on through much remembered allotments with their tomatoes, rickety sheds, trellises holding up wind battered runner beans and bottles on sticks to scare the birds and made our way slowly down towards the canal.

'Greta use to spend all her days down here' said Lillian. 'Whilst I played with dolls and Joan (their elder sister) did her thing, Greta would disappear down here from breakfast until dinnertime getting up to all sorts of mischief, she was a very naughty girl!.' My brother and I were beginning to understand where all our mischievousness had come from. We had always assumed it was from Dad, full of wit and ever up for a laugh at someone else's expense; but the real (had they had CCTV when we were growing up we would have spent many a happy year in Borstal) mischief genes we could at last thankfully blame on having been inherited from Mum.

We stood and looked at the view. Nothing much had changed; canals seldom do. The gasworks opposite had gone and in the distance instead was the Leicester City football ground; the engine sheds on the left hand side had gone and the factories were boarded up and in disuse. But the canal was exactly the same as it was when it was built and you didn't need much imagination to picture the whole scene as it had been when I was a boy and how it must have been in the thirties when Mum was dicing with death as a little kid.

We turned right and walked along the tow-path. There was the massive weir I remember being terrified of as a child. There had been a half submerged rowing boat caught against the underground wall just before the water fell in a torrent into the lake beyond. We used to imagine children and their father had been in that boat and how they had been swept away and drowned. I could picture the little children caught beneath the water, tangled up in weed with their feet trapped by old prams and bicycles, the precious air being forced from their bodies as they changed from children of this World to water babies, never to be seen again – a recurring theme for me it seems. Further along the tow-path narrowed to become a rickety iron gantry. It was only four feet to cross but beneath the gantry the water churned down through a small arch and into one of the disused factories. It was still as dangerous as a mill race but back then there was the added horror of turbine blades powering factory machinery which would have chopped you to pieces had you slipped through the widely spaced railings as you crossed the metal grill. I shuddered to think that we were all allowed to play there with no supervision, constantly daring each other to undertake ever more risky escapades.

Then we came to the lock where we had decided to say goodbye to Mum. The lock itself had recently been repaired, had two sets of gates, the upstream ones of which were open, and on the other side of the canal someone had planted a flowerbed and repainted the sign which quite by chance aptly read 'St. Margaret's Lock'. Downstream of the lock was the dilapidated factory area we had walked through, but upstream the scenery gave way to fields and woodland and made for a very pleasant spot for our ceremony. We had decided to take it in turns to tip the ash pellets from the urn into the water and then sink the urn with the residue in the lock itself.

I think I said a few solemn words for us all and then commenced the tipping process, followed by Paul, then by Lillian, when all of a sudden Alex shouted in a panicked voice,

'The ducks are coming! The ducks are coming!' Sure enough swimming madly towards the lock from the upstream direction and in great excitement was a squadron of Mallards in v-shaped formation, led by a jubilant drake, and all of them laughing as only ducks can. Reacting swiftly, Alex tried to swing the gates to the lock closed but could only shut the gate on our side of the canal. In came the duck-party making a most grateful commotion, and within seconds any of Mum's pellets on the surface had been devoured by the leading party-goers, the remaining guests either busily diving down to salvage what they could from the depths, or bobbing stupidly upside down and waggling their bottoms in the air. We all stood aghast and watched the feast in complete helplessness.

Our horror however quickly turned to amusement, and knowing that Mum would have found the situation equally hilarious, we actively fed the rest of Margaret to the now expectant and maniacally hooting ducks and threw the urn into the canal. This being made of 'bronzed plastic' failed to sink, so we had to search for a long stick to bash the urn, which still failed to submerge it, and then find stones to throw at the urn until it finally and slowly disappeared beneath the surface. I am sure if anyone had been watching a sombrely dressed family chucking rocks into the canal including some elderly people, one of whom seemed to be bashing the water with a branch whilst shouting, and had known this was part of a farewell ceremony to a loved one, they would have either thought us completely barmy or have called the police.

This was my third time in the capacity as 'Ash-master', and I have to admit to never having been that lucky or successful. The first time I was awarded this highly distinguished and responsible role was after the death of my father. At the time my parents had been living on the sixth floor of a block of sea-front apartments overlooking the West Pier in Brighton (or 'West Pie' as it had become following endless storms, neglect, and a suspicious fire, the large red 'R' having given up illuminating the countless starlings which sweep majestically across the skies in a fantasia of formations at dusk). They had fallen in love with the pier following the film *Oh! What a Lovely War!* which was staged there in 1967 and had resulted in the pier being transformed into a white beauty of Victorian engineering reminiscent of a Christmas cake - (but without a giant plastic bride and her inevitably ginger haired groom being stuck on top). Having spent twenty years living opposite what was becoming a poor reflection of its former self, Mum decided that it would be nice for Dad's ashes to adorn the wreckage so she would be able to sit in the window and reminisce. Although the pier was now closed to the public this posed no problem as my brother had his pilot's licence, and we decided to fly past the following day at a set time and scatter Dad's ashes over the pier from above.

Tea-time the next day, we took off in a hired two-seater Cessna aircraft from nearby Shoreham airport with my brother at the controls and me in the co-pilot seat, and in charge of the 'bronze plastic' urn. The Cessna is ideal for what we had in mind as it has the wing above the cockpit, so it would be easy for me to see the target pier below and tip Dad out as we flew by. Mum meantime was ready by the window in her flat with a glass of champagne, some very close family, and a pair of binoculars.

Within minutes of leaving Shoreham we were over the target area, but my brother being a closet 'I wish I had been in the Second World War' pilot, we weren't ready to start the official ceremony until the Cessna had become a temporary 'Squadron 633 Mosquito'. We first flew past the pier at just above sea level with sea-spray actually hitting the windscreen, then arose to a few thousand feet to do a few massive show-off and noisy spins, and then dived back down towards the pier at breakneck speed with my evil-grinning brother pulling back on the column just short of the wings folding back and us plummeting into the ocean. The improvised air-show being temporarily put on hold, we now lined up for an approach at a highly illegal altitude of some fifty feet above the pier and low enough so that Mum could actually look down on the proceedings. It may be worth saying at this stage that we had obtained permission to drop the ashes from the local Air Authority on the strict basis that we would not descend to less than one thousand feet, and that the urn would be returned safely to the airfield otherwise having been deemed to be a bomb if allowed to drop from the aircraft.

By now I was coated in sweat not only from the heat in the cockpit but from the sheer terror of being a reluctant participant in the air-show, but I nevertheless managed to open the aircraft window, opened the lid of the urn and made ready to spill the contents. As my brother shouted 'Now!' and banked towards the coast, I moved the urn to the window and tried to thrust out 'hand and urn' as one.

This being supposedly a book with a science flavour, this particular escapade is something you can experiment with yourself. Next time you are in the passenger seat of the car, and it is safe to do so, ask the driver to speed up to 100 mph, then open the window and hold outside a plastic beaker of sand. What you will probably find is that a) it is almost impossible to hold your hand steady at this speed given normal human muscle power, b) the shaking beaker thus develops a seemingly mind of its own assuming you can hold on to it; and c) the contents are more likely to be blasted back through the open window by the thrust of the air than to fall to the road in a nice orderly fashion. It is actually quite basic physics of course, and easy to determine the exact likely outcome of all this given sufficient time, the relevant textbooks and equipment, and a convenient laboratory incorporating a wind-tunnel, coupled with some preferably female undergraduate assistants in white coats.

Through her binoculars my mother saw my brother and I become an instant minstrel duet as the black ash filled the cockpit and stuck fast to our sweat-soaked grinning faces.

As she fell to the floor of her flat in hysterical laughter, my temporarily blinded brother meanwhile battled to keep the plane on a straight and level course at so low an altitude and in a cockpit full of ash, and I tried to not swallow or blink into my eyes too much of my recently departed parent.

Needless to say we had to make another circuit. This time all we could do was scrape off as much of Dad as we could with our fingers and flick the residue out of the window; hardly dignified. I also tried to empty the rest of the urn but this was swept from my hands and, much against above-mentioned regulations, dropped as a bronze-cased bomb into the sea. First attempt as Ash-master? – Failed!

My second attempt followed the drowning at sea of my wife's father Nicky, whilst they were on holiday in The Gambia. His widow, Mary, having repatriated his body decided that as he had spent much of his life as a fisherman working off Brighton, we should scatter his ashes in the sea off that particular coast.

As luck had it, an old fisherman friend of Nicky's was happy to take us out for our ceremony in his old-fashioned fishing boat nestled safely in Brighton marina. The boat was fairly small with just enough room for the skipper in the wheelhouse, so the seven or so of us in the party had to stand on deck and hold tight to the railings.

As luck didn't have it, the day we had chosen heralded one of the worst storms of the year on the south coast of England. The second we left the calm marina waters and passed through the huge concrete passage into the sea itself, the boat was tossed about like something horrible that floats when you flush the toilet, and us along with it.

It's very exciting to be at sea in a fishing boat for the first time, braving the weather by holding on for dear life and bracing yourself against the incoming spray and gale force winds, getting soaked to the skin, riding the peaks and troughs of the mountainous waves and staring ahead at an ever darkening and more foreboding horizon. You may recall a Fry's chocolate bar from the 1970's called Five Boy's which depicted the face of a young man in five different attitudes as he tasted and consumed his favourite sweet. After about a minute, my expression of excitement quickly turned to one of concern; to foreboding; to dread in the sure knowledge we were all going to join Nicky in death; and finally to the idiot look when you are past all hope, so what does it matter anyway!

I grabbed Mary, pulled her to the front of the vessel, and made ready to scatter Nicky's remains. Being a non-swimmer who has never felt comfortable with the sea, Mary nevertheless bravely allowed herself to be put under my wing. The rest of the party were by now cowering as best they could behind the wheelhouse. Mary and I now tried to make it plain that we were about to start the ceremony, but the howling wind made any possibility of communication hopeless. So off came the lid, off flew the lid, out flew the ash, off flew the urn, and we turned to see everyone else covered in what would more recently have been blamed on an Icelandic ash cloud. Second attempt as Ash-master? – Failed!

I am doing something today I never thought I would catch myself doing ever again; and that is going to school by train - on a Saturday. I have with me my grown-up's satchel containing pens; my trusty calculator; an exercise book; a text book entitled *volcanoes, earthquakes and tsunamis*; and my packed lunch. All it lacks to be just like the juvenile equivalent from my teenage years, is a packet of 'Lucky Strike' cigarettes, a stolen lighter, some spray paint, and a can of cider. This is of course 'big school', and all my fellow pupils will be adult. But nevertheless we are supposed to behave sensibly, respect our tutor, and most importantly, turn up on time. I can just about manage the first two of these directives if I try really hard, but unfortunately will fail on the third count, because my rail journey has been part replaced by a bus service, due to weekend engineering work. As my few fellow passengers and I are marshalled out of the train and led towards an old-fashioned bus waiting outside one of the village stations en route, I replace my frustration with a sense of excitement. This is just the sort of bus I travelled on as a little kid, and I eagerly make my way to the top deck, hoping to nab one of the front window seats all to myself. Achieving my aim, I sit back and thrill to the familiar sights and smells of a bus dating from the 1950's. The seats have what was once a thick green and gold flecked velvet-like covering, and are spacious; the walls are a subdued cream melamine finish; the handrails are polished chrome but with a touch of the underlying metal showing through; the naked light-bulbs are the type which can be easily removed; there is an overhead cord to pull to request a stop; and there is a large round fish-eye mirror, for the driver to see what mischief is afoot upstairs. Even the condition of this aged workhorse is acceptable, given it having been relegated to ferrying school-children and occasional 'rail-replacement service' use. Refreshingly there is no CCTV; no restrictive seatbelts; no health and safety signs telling you all the dirty and disgusting things you are not allowed to do; and no travel insurance advertisements. Before we set off a very little boy comes and sits next to me, and his mother asks if I would keep an eye on him whilst she brings her bags upstairs.

'We will have to hold tight to the front rail', I tell him as the bus starts to move; and his knuckles turn white as he clutches the rail as if his life depended on it.

The great thing about these journeys is that they follow a 'mystery' route not normally taken by buses, and certainly not by a huge double-decked monster with a roaring engine, belching diesel fumes. As we speed down narrow lanes and by-ways, it is wonderful to see the attention we are attracting, not only from passers-by but from people actually coming out of their homes to see this unexpected interloper; spoiling the morning's harmony, but at the same time injecting something out of the ordinary to the day. Sitting at the front, the

216

perspective you get makes the bus seem much wider than it really is, and the white knuckle boy and I are both constantly ducking as lamp-posts and trees seemingly fly towards us on an inevitable collision path. Every now and then an overhanging branch will swat the window with a tremendous 'thwak', making us jump and laugh, and we cover our faces, expecting to be showered in glass. We also take sudden corners, as if the driver himself is unsure of the switchback route, and are thrown from side to side with glee. After a few of these episodes however, white knuckle boy's far too protective mother (and much to both our dismay), insists on him going to sit with her further back, where he will be safer under her wing. As I watch him totter mournfully down the aisle, I think back to a very special bus trip I made, when I was about his age...

THE INCREDIBLE JOURNEY

When I was five years old the World seemed a very safe place. I remember sometimes walking the two miles or so from our house into Beckenham High Street and catching a big red double-decker bus to the next town, Bromley. There, I would walk into Dunn's, the large department store which was right next to the bus stop so I couldn't get lost, head up to the waitress silver service lounge cafeteria where I had been with Mother, and order a pot of tea and a hot buttered tea-cake. I would sit at my table for ages feeling very grown up in my velvet shorts and black school blazer (even though it was the holidays), and watch the other people coming and going all the while wondering what was in the parcels they had purchased. I remember that the waitresses were always neatly dressed in black with white aprons and hats, were very polite but very old, and always careful with the silver cutlery which must have been real solid silver and worth millions of pounds. They were especially careful to keep an eye trained on this strange little boy bereft of adult supervision, to ensure none of this treasure found its way into his green tartan duffle bag; which unbeknown to them, contained a Tupperware flask of weak orange squash; bits of sandwich; a Fry's Five Boys chocolate bar; a picture book of trains; a compass I didn't know I didn't know how to use; and a stuffed toy dog suffering from too many haircuts - and which followed me wherever I went. When it came to pay I would hand over one of the huge half-crown pieces I had received for Christmas as if it was a golden doubloon, not quite understanding how money worked or what change to expect but somehow knowing this would be more than enough and would still provide sufficient funds for the bus fare back home. Sometimes Mother would ask where I had been all morning and I would tell her honestly, receiving the half-hearted reply 'that's nice dear' as she carried on with whatever it was she was doing, having taken no notice of my attire or the duffle bag held nonchalantly in 'Dick Whittington' fashion over my shoulder.

Just once, whilst waiting outside Dunn's for the big red double-decker bus back to Beckenham after my tea and cake, I saw pulling up an incredible, magical, shiny-new Greenline bus. I had never been on one of these leviathans but I knew by the gold lettering they were special, and by the luscious green colour that they went beyond the towns and into the wide open countryside. The sense of adventure as I was magnetized aboard was immense.

The interior of the Greenline was much plusher than the red buses and smelled to me of freshly polished woodwork, mown grass and sunshine. There were pictures depicting unknown country destinations, which to my eager eyes may as well have been far off foreign shores yet to be discovered and where man had yet to set foot, even the passengers on board seemed to be dressed for a long and arduous journey into the unknown. I took my seat at the rear of the Greenline and peered expectantly through the window. Of course I had no idea where I was going apart from on an adventure to probably somewhere with a magically sounding name, the likes of which I had only read about in stories by Rudyard Kipling or my brothers' *Eagle* comic. When the kindly looking conductor approached me I held out all the change I had left, and asked to be taken as far as that would allow me, as long as it would also get me home again. I explained that:

'I was on an adventure; had a compass with me if he needed to borrow it; and that I wouldn't be missed until tea-time', although I wasn't sure what time that was, and in any event didn't have a watch, and wasn't very good at telling the time anyway having been confused by an uncle insisting on explaining the twenty-four hour clock to me, which left me muddled for many a year. When you are five, being admonished for saying one o'clock when clearly you mean thirteen hundred hours can be quite disconcerting.

The kindly looking conductor led me to the front of the Greenline where he could keep a watchful eye on me, and 'make sure no wild animals get you' he said, and after printing me off a ticket from the magical silver box hanging on his chest, left me to watch the world change shape. Before long we started to leave the towns behind, to be replaced by fields with animals, and the occasional village. The streetlamps disappeared to be replaced by rows of trees, and the busy traffic became an occasional car or bicycle. As time ticked on by and familiarity fell away on our journey to the edge of the known world, the sheer scale of my undertaking became somewhat daunting. Although it was great fun and so exciting seeing all these new sights, I began to realise that once I got off the Greenline my supplies were unlikely to last that long. I had no money left; my toy dog - although a great comfort, was no canine Pegasus to fly me home; and all that tea I had drunk meant I now desperately needed a pee, and was far too shy to say anything.

Somehow, it may have been the look on my face or just the tears, I don't know; the kindly looking conductor understood my plight. At the next stop, he took me across the road to the opposing bus-stop, gave me a written note with the number bus I would need to catch, together with a note of explanation for his counterpart conductor; and left me feeling much happier but quite alone by the side of the road. There were some handy bushes nearby, so I made myself comfortable, worked my way through the supplies in my duffle-bag and sat on the kerbside to wait for another Greenline home. It is amazing how noisy the quiet countryside can be when you are really young, especially if you only have your imagination and a hairless stuffed dog as companions. How, once you get used to the rustle of the leaves in the trees, and the hum of the insects, you can hear but not quite see huge creatures moving about in the trees across the road, which must be either Lions, Tigers or Bears oh no! How simple rolling hills take on the majesty of mountains, and it is so dark in the thick forest beyond, that it must be Africa over there and the deep mysterious Congo where head-hunters, pygmies, and huge black men with spears live, who eat small boys foolish enough to stray far from home all by themselves. Even the sky seems to close in and the clouds take on fearsome shapes you daren't put names to; and always, always there is someone or something behind you that you can sense, but isn't there when you peek bravely over your shoulder. And you think of things you shouldn't be thinking of when you are only little and all alone.

There used to be a ride called the 'World Cruise' at Battersea funfair in South London, before the whole park closed not long after lots of children died on the big dipper. The World Cruise was simply a current-

driven boat ride through dark and twisting caverns, past glass fronted displays depicting lifelike but fantastical scenes from different continents. The little boats only held two people and were so shallow that if anyone rocked the boat the murky water would lap over the top and threaten to sink you, which was very scary for a little boy. Even more scary were the passages that appeared endless and seemed to go off as if to nowhere, or were blocked by a part submerged door, and you knew (because your brother had told you), that if your boat turned down one of these by mistake, you would plummet down to the underworld as if this was the river Styx itself. But most scary of all and definitely the food for nightmares, was the display cabinet representing darkest Africa. Strange jungle noises emanated from the dense water-dripping forest, and large snakes, bigger than the biggest ever man, draped and hissed from the branches; but peering from behind the larger trees were fearsome black men wearing necklaces of teeth, and bones through their noses, and belts made from human hands, and yellow glass eyes that followed you, and stared at you even if you closed your own eyes tight shut, and pulled your jumper over your head, and wished and wished the ride was over - so you could go on it again.

But eventually I heard the welcome chug of a Greenline approaching, and so wearily and gratefully made my way home, still taking the occasional glance back at this strange land. By the time I neared where I lived and was on familiar territory however, I began to

223

feel braver. I was quite convinced I had been at least half way round the World; and that had I actually come face to face with any foes, monsters or giants, I would have conquered all. But when later, I proudly and excitedly told Mother of my 'incredible journey', the only discernible change to her 'that's nice dear', was that when I went to bed that night, Rudyard Kipling's picture-filled *Adventure Stories* that had lain next to the torch on my bedside table, had been displaced by *Noddy in Toyland.*

I am back on the late morning train once again,
but this time all is chaos. The train before was cancelled
(which makes me glad I didn't rush to catch that one);
but everyone who did rush to catch that one, is now on
this one as well, and there is consequently insufficient
space. I am standing, along with crowds of others, but
have managed to find a precarious perch on which to rest
my current science book, that at the same time leaves
one hand free to make notes. Today's subject is based
around the story of a glass of water and threatens to be
interesting, but there is a commotion that draws my
attention. Further down the carriage, two buxom ladies
wearing hats, are pointing at something awful and
calling loudly for the ticket inspector to be found. Being
naturally inquisitive, I surreptitiously move as close as
the crowded carriage will allow, and espy the source of
the ladies' disquiet. There, lying across two seats and
obviously either asleep, or in a drunken stupor, or both,
is a counterpart 'Unlikely Gentleman'. He is not of
course my 'Unlikely Gentleman' because **he** travels on
my old line, but this one is sufficiently unsavoury to act
as an adequate surrogate. In striving to listen in to the
ladies' conversation, I learn that the counterpart has
committed five crimes in their eyes, which is why they
are so outraged. Firstly he is taking up two seats;
secondly he should not be on a seat anyway as they are

225

having to stand up – so he is ill-mannered; thirdly he looks distinctly unpleasant – a dreadful crime in itself; fourthly he looks so distinctly unpleasant he probably hasn't got a ticket; and worst of all, he is in the 'priority seats' set aside for the elderly, the disabled, women with or about to be with child; or if there are none of these classes of individual present, buxom ladies in hats.

I for one would never contemplate sitting in a 'priority seat', but that is because my dearly departed Mother drummed into me that such seating being set aside for the elderly, they are likely to be wet, or at the very least damp. She found this out to her cost travelling by bus in Brighton one day; sitting on a priority seat near the driver and wondering if the bus company had installed heated seats, until a too horrible to contemplate dampness started to seep through to her buttocks. All such seats have ever since been known in my family as the 'wet seats'. If this sounds paranoid, have a look at such seats next time you travel by public transport, and see if you also notice the plush of the fabric to be a darker shade than other normal seats; and let us see if you dare touch the seat to see if it is cold and dry, or still slightly warm and urine soaked. My eldest daughter was disbelieving and ignored the family warning, until she too fell foul of this incontinence trap, and had to suffer the ignominy of walking home in tears, in an obviously sodden skirt, to sterilise herself and change clothes.

As the counterpart is obviously not going to wake up, and even if he did, as he is obviously not going to apologise and kindly offer his two 'wet seats' to the buxom hats, I return my attention to my rather appropriate, hypothetical glass of water.

Even I learnt at school that water is made up of molecules consisting of hydrogen and oxygen atoms, and that water is essential to all life as we know it. I think we have all also heard the tale that as water is forever recycled, we could be drinking dinosaur pee (which is not strictly true by the way). But can you answer the logic defying question as to why solid water (ice), floats on liquid water? Or did you know that steam is invisible? Or do you know how sweat cools you down? It is easy to think of water molecules as the tiny droplets of water you can just about see as condensation, but in fact in my imaginary glass of water there are a **lot** of molecules. If every human on the planet could gather round my glass, and each count a different share of the molecules at the rate of one molecule per second, it would take ten million years to count all the molecules in that one glass. There is also a lot of energy in that glass. Scientists are very near to creating a nuclear fusion reactor. What this essentially does is recreate the power of a hydrogen bomb but in something we can control and use peacefully, and with little or no by-product other than oxygen. It fuses together the hydrogen atoms in my water glass at incredibly high temperatures, creating helium, and in so doing releases vast amounts of energy. In fact in one litre of water, there is enough hydrogen to create the equivalent energy output from 25 million litres of oil. Once the clever scientists perfect their technique, and then the clever Chinese engineers miniaturise the process, it will effectively change World dynamics within a very short space of time. Imagine everyone having access to limitless power, at next to nothing cost; no more reliance on fossil fuels; a massive reduction in Global pollution; and no more being held to ransom by oil-producing countries!

But all this talk of water and incontinence is making **me** want a pee, and there is no way I can possibly make my way to a toilet on such a crowded train. I will have to close my eyes, jiggle around a bit, and think of something else instead. I could start by recalling another time, and another place involving buxom ladies in hats; but somehow I don't think it's going to help…

HOMESTAY

Some fifty years after my 'incredible journey', here was I with my wife stepping off another bus onto the banks of magical-sounding Lake Titicaca, on a **real** adventure that would take us to the snow-line of volcanic Mount Cotopaxi; deep into the Amazon basin; to experience the majesty of Machu Picchu; and to follow in the footsteps of Charles Darwin in the Galapagos.

(By the way, if you decide to go to Machu Picchu, don't do the mammoth trek that all the back-packers do, there is a posh train that will take you there

instead. You can sit back and relax; enjoy a waiter service luncheon; and wave at all the long-faced walkers as they plod forever onwards; all of them inwardly dreading the communal toilet stops where nothing ever flushes away and a seat is an unfulfilled dream.)

Lake Titicaca sits in a basin within the high Andes Mountains, an enormous chain of extinct and active volcanoes that stretches along the West coast of South America. Heralded as the highest navigable lake on the planet because it is large enough and deep enough to have some big boats plying it, it is bordered by Peru and Bolivia and is found at the impressive height of 12,500 feet (3,800 metres) above sea level. This is three times higher than the tallest mountain in Britain; higher than the highest capital city in the World; and higher than the Peruvian city of Cusco, once the capital of the Inca civilization, and where today young priests try and sell you oxygen as you sit and marvel at the splendour inside the Spanish built Cathedral.

All the guide books recommend you take time to acclimatise to altitude, reaching the height of Titicaca steadily over the period of a few days. This advice was of no use to us however, as we had arrived there directly from sea-level after a few hours bus-ride and we now waited, feeling light-headed and short of breath for the boat which would take us to our island for the night; and our much vaunted (in the guide) and much dreaded (by us) - Homestay!

As our boat crossed the lake, despite enjoying the fantastic scenery, which consists mostly of beautiful snow-capped volcanic peaks and their mirror images reflected in the pure mountain waters, we found the climate at this altitude disconcerting. When the Sun was shining it was quite warm and we could sit in just a sweater enjoying the exceptionally bright sunlight on our faces. As soon as the Sun disappeared behind a cloud however, within seconds it was absolutely freezing, requiring the putting on and hiding our heads and hands within the folds of our coats, as despite many attempts, we were yet to be sold any 'genuine alpaca' acrylic gloves, hats and wraps. Of course, the cloud only lasted a minute or two after which the Sun would burst forth, we would get too hot and take our coats off, and the cycle would start again as the next cloud created obscurity. After half an hour of this we were not only feeling jet-lagged; exhausted; altitude-sick and a little queasy from the motion of the boat; we were also coated in a film of cold sweat. What delight we consequently felt when we finally approached the island where we would be spending the night, and saw waiting for us on the quay, a line of very large looking, colourful blanket clad women in pork pie hats. One of those hats would be selecting us and putting us under her wing, and in our bedraggled state we really felt like little evacuees finding refuge and solace in this far flung corner of the World. We were even wearing labels with our names on in chubby pencil! Which particular hat would choose us we had no idea but as advised by our travel agent, we had come prepared with a large carrier bag full of fruit, bread, biscuits, chocolate and other goodies for our 'homestay' family; and had been assured that our surrogate mother would carry our bags for us up to our temporary home. We had also been provided with a sheet of paper listing a dozen useful but unpronounceable words in Quechua, the only language the hats spoke; but unhelpfully also listing the Spanish equivalent, a language **we** didn't speak – what joy!

Thus armed with baggage, goodies and our less than handy sheet we disembarked with our fellow explorers on the pretty alpine-style island and waited to be selected, trying not to catch the eye of some of the grumpier looking women or to be honest; the more smelly looking.

Within minutes, a very rotund obstacle approached covered in a mountain of predominantly red-hued blanketry, out of the top of which popped a matching red-hued jolly face with beaming, glistening eyes and topped off with some dark curls under a somewhat listless and battered pork pie hat. I could immediately see that the beaming, glistening eyes were somewhat transfixed by the very large carrier I was holding, and this is what had singled us out from our fellows. Indeed within seconds, a hand appeared from under the blanketry as if from nowhere; the carrier was grabbed, and she was off; beckoning us to follow and leaving us to the porterage.

Fearful we would lose sight of our blanket-lady we hurried after her trying to identify some unique feature that would make her stand out from the others should we become separated, which from behind was impossible. Very soon however she came to a few stone steps leading up from the quayside and turned to smile and stamp her foot by way of encouragement. As we started up the few steps we noticed they wound round a corner, which on reaching led to another flight of steps leading round another corner; a process that kept repeating itself as the steps wound their way around and steadily vertically up the island. Somewhat dismayed at having to climb steps in our condition and with the bags as an additional burden, every time we came to a corner and stopped to recover ourselves we lost sight of blanket-lady and had to speed up for the next section. I am sure that the island really was rather pretty and that the views of the lake as we climbed were breathtaking but we had no breath left to take. Had we known at that stage that the village, our destination, was at the top of the island and that the island was one thousand foot high, and steps all the way, I think we would have thrown ourselves off a cliff. As it was, half way up my wife desperately needed a pee (an effect of altitude sickness), and using sign language to explain the necessity to a horribly grubby urchin sitting on a wall and amusedly watching the idiot foreigners on their weekly struggle up the mountain, she was shown into a stinking hut. I meantime was nearly dead from thirst and indicated as much to the horribly grubby urchin who disappeared and returned with a filthy plastic bottle of water, for which he demanded one dollar holding out a snot covered hand in expectation. The transaction duly undertaken I drank some of the water, immediately threw up, and thus felt more thirsty than ever and looked around for somewhere convenient to die.

Eventually we neared the summit, the temperature only having dropped a few more degrees in this time, and saw blanket-lady waiting for us chatting to some older blanket people, and a donkey which I remember cursing under my breath and thinking it could have carried the bags for us. Blanket-lady was clearly amused at something and kept shaking the carrier, then pointing in our direction and laughing with her friends, but although we could not see anyone in a clowns outfit following behind us, I am sure she would have been too polite to actually laugh at us. The afore-mentioned donkey by the way must have been telepathic and multi-lingual because he started towards me as I took the final few steps to the top, and decided to squeeze through a narrow stone gateway at the same time as me, forcing me painfully against the wall, covering me in slimy donkey sweat and treading on a foot - more mirth from the 'too polite' blanket folk.

Feeling like donkeys ourselves we were led to one of many stone houses, up some external wooden rickety stairs, and to a room with a wooden floor, wooden beams, a wooden bed, and a thousand blankets; and sort of pushed inside to make ourselves at home. By now it was freezing cold; we both felt physically ill and so lay down on the bed having covered ourselves in as many blankets as possible and trembled ourselves back to life. After some time had passed, blanket-lady came in and summoned us to follow her downstairs. On the way she pointed out a wooden privy at the bottom of a rubble and junk strewn courtyard, making squatting gestures to indicate its' purpose, and then led us into the main room

234

of her home which was magically warm with a raging fire. The room obviously doubled up as kitchen, living room, and dining room, and in the corner on a bench sat a man (we assumed him to be her husband), looking very as you might expect an indigenous South American to look – all dark skin; heavily wrinkled, rugged, weather-beaten face; jet black hair and dark glowing eyes; wearing a black suit turned shiny with age and wear, a greasy red neckerchief, and a battered homburg hat. If he had been picking his teeth with a stiletto and nursing a shotgun on his lap, the picture would have been complete.

Blanket-lady had by now shed a few layers and was looking a little younger than we had imagined, and had a similar look to her husband although a much fuller and rosier face, with dumpling cheeks. My wife and I did some polite bowing and nodding, and I made a short 'how welcome we feel' speech in 'English for the deaf', which they didn't understand a word of but seemed to enjoy, and we sat down to eat a bowl of genuine 'homestay' gruel; doing lots more nodding, 'ahhing', and rubbing our tummies. There was of course no sign of the wholesome food we had brought! Now, as happens anywhere on the planet in such a situation, during the meal (which both blanket-lady and glowing-eyes preferred to watch us eat rather than partake) a young boy entered, obviously the son of the house, and stood in front of us brandishing an indigenous South American version of – a recorder. After much pushing from the blanket mother and growling from the glowing-eye father, the boy began to play an unknown song quite as badly as any European kid can play a well-known melody, but much to his parent's and therefore our feigned delight; and kept playing until with a smile on my face and showing otherwise sentiment, I paid him a couple of dollars to shut up and go away.

Now like a couple of naughty babies it was mimicked that we should go and have a sleep until the clock struck something or other, and we were packed off to our bedroom which we realised was above the main room of the house.

As we lay under our mound of blankets and wondered about our adventure so far we spotted the only adornment in the room which was a small stick, tied up with a bit of string and nailed to the wall. We wondered about this for a long time and concluded that either our hosts were stick worshippers, or that this was a 'lucky stick', or it was somehow holding the house up – we will never know.

It was now dark outside, extremely cold, and we were exhausted; a good long sleep would have suited us fine until next morning. We forgot that we were on an organised holiday, we had chosen the boy-scout version, and 'every moment of every day will be filled with a new and wonderful experience!'

Sure enough, the door opens and in comes blanket-lady and takes my wife away. In the meantime glowing eyes comes in and throws a Clint Eastwood style poncho over my head, on top of which he plants and tries to sell me a smelly woollen hat with earpieces.

Seconds later in comes blanket-lady again, this time leading a miniature western version of herself, but also with an earpiece hat, and it is my wife! We are off to a dance – how wonderful! We are in raptures! It's just what we needed!

It seems all us explorers have been invited (forced) to attend the dance, as we meet many other similarly attired couples as we are led by our blanket-women to the central village hall (corrugated iron hut). It seems that real men like old glowing-eyes don't do dancing, instead they seem to gather in small groups, smoke a lot, and leer at us foreign interlopers, probably wondering how much bounty we are worth.

The hall itself has been aesthetically lit inside with as many stark fluorescent tubes as it will accommodate, and is guaranteed to give you eye-ache within thirty seconds of entering; but there is a smart six piece band, and a table where you can purchase much needed water and local beer. As we all pack inside for warmth, we note that my wife and I are far from being the only explorers looking less than at their best. Unlike a western disco however, there is no time to mingle, watch proceedings and stand around trying to look cool in the cowboy poncho with silly hat. The band swiftly starts up, it is not a tune we know; but all the blanket ladies grab the western versions of themselves, my wife included; and the dancing begins.

Fortunately you don't need to know the steps for dancing at a blanket event. My wife's hands are gripped tightly, and an endless spinning commences. Round and round go blanket-lady and my wife; round and round go the other couples; round and round go my eyes as I watch and become dizzy, and as the harsh lights create swirling circles on the polished lino floor. At last however the music slows down and stops; my wife's face is white as a sheet, she stumbles towards a chair and I bend over her to see if she is dying. But the music starts again; a shadow approaches; it is our beaming blanket-lady. She grabs my arms, we move onto the floor, and it is my turn to go round and round; but this time seeing the walls and exhausted onlookers flash constantly past as we turn, turn, turn on this carousel of misery. The tune goes on forever; the blanket-lady is grinning at me; nodding encouragement and loving every second of this torture. Perhaps she is getting her own back for all the torment the Inquisition gave her forebears under ancient Spanish rule; but at last the music dies down and I stand unsteadily on my feet breathing hard and gasping for oxygen. But look, why stop now? We are all forming a giant circle around the room, everyone has to join and hold hands with their neighbours, and now we are **all** beginning to go round and round, faster and faster; not using any dancing steps or moving to any recognisable beat; just running faster and faster in one huge great screaming circle; around and around, driven by the madly laughing blanket women; the band bashing away on their instruments for all their worth; faster and faster; all the explorers screaming; and no-one daring to let go for fear of been thrown into outer space by the momentum.

(They used to have a machine like this at Battersea Fun-Fair in the sixties called the Rotor. It also went round and round and as it accelerated you stuck to the walls, the floor fell away and you were left suspended in mid air, also screaming and expecting to fall to your death if the machine broke.)

Eventually our blanket driven rotor slowed down, my wife and I teetered towards our seats for much needed rest and water, and the band took a break. But oh no; another band has started up at the other end of the hall; the blanket lady grabs my arms and as I stare appealingly towards my withering wife, I am dragged onto the floor for another spin-cycle at one thousand revolutions per minute.

Finally, people begin to be helped away - some of them crying; some being literally dragged, and we feel it wouldn't be too rude to make the sign of needing to go to sleep, and hope our blanket-lady will take us home.

She certainly seems reluctant to leave this revelry, but thankfully leads us through the pitch darkness and icy cold to her home, and up the rickety stairs to our room where she gives us a lighted candle to help us see ourselves to bed; the electric generator having been turned off for the night. Smothered in blankets, utterly spent, and craving sleep, I exhale a stream of ice crystals to extinguish our little light, smile at the faint shaft of moonlight playing on the lucky stick in the cold night air, and hope it will soon be day two of our adventure. It is now so quiet and dark and peaceful, surely nothing can disturb my repose. Everyone is asleep; everything is asleep; my eyes feel heavier and heavier, my breathing becomes slower and steadier and I feel myself sinking into a deep calm. Hush.

My wife needs a pee. She suddenly realises she is desperate for a pee. She didn't go earlier because the hut on the hill was disgusting and the toilet in the courtyard at the blanket-lady's house didn't have a door. She pulls the blankets off us both and she gets up; and despite the cold she starts to dance the dance we all do when we try to stop ourselves peeing and know the cause is lost. The family downstairs will hear her; I can't take her into the courtyard to the privy as it is too cold, too dark and too dangerous on the icy steps; and in any case we don't have a torch. And in any case we don't have any matches for the candle; and in any case I can't even see the damn door! In desperation I search for a receptacle, but apart from the lucky stick I know there is nothing in the room. Then, under the bed I find what feels like a child's plastic potty.

'This will have to do' I declare in triumph.

It does do, but the trickle I hear (which is more a torrent), does not stop. How much can the potty take? What if it was to overflow and something spilt through the boards into the room below where the family are sleeping? We can't see how full it is getting. I desperately search again under the bed, and this time find what feels like another but much smaller plastic child's potty. We organise an exchange at a critical point and the trickling continues into the new vessel, but thankfully dies away before I have to contemplate even more desperate measures. Now of course, all that trickling sound as any gentleman will know, means I desperately need a pee. I kneel before where I can feel the potties are and try sensing how much room there is in each, but my fingers are numb with cold and I can't stop shivering so I just have to do what I can and hope for the best.

In the cold light of morning, I am to be seen on the rickety ice-laden wooden stairs balancing two completely brimming potties; and with difficulty making my way down to the privy in the courtyard, trying not to spill any of the contents. Indeed, I am to be seen by old glowing-eyes who is also up early. He approaches, and obviously and kindly wants to help, and he tries to take the potties off me. He is smiling, scowling, and grinning all at the same time which makes for an interesting visage. I try to stop him and pull away nodding 'no' with my head; he tries harder to help and pulls at my arms nodding 'yes' with his head - it does not end well!

It is evening, it is nearly Christmas again, and I am on my way home from the City. I have had my exam results and I am doing surprisingly well. One more year of study and I will actually be a Bachelor of Science, I then have to decide on a topic to focus on for my honours. I was consequently feeling pleased with myself this morning, and I decided to throw some money away and caution to the wind by treating myself for once to a first class return ticket. Travelling 'posh' didn't really make much difference on the way to London Bridge, as I always manage to get a seat with a table to work at anyway. The real bonus was to be a guaranteed space in the plush first class compartment on this train home; and a seat away from the hoi polloi.

So here I am; it is evening, it is nearly Christmas again, and if I could see my face reflected in the dark window I would observe evolving expressions of annoyance; frustration; anger; hate; and sheer murder. I am having to stand because all the first class seats are taken, and despite my ardent prayers there is no sign of a ticket inspector. Looking around me I can clearly see that most if not all of the people sitting in **my** seat are not of first class calibre. Take for example the young black couple with the little child and the suitcases. They are probably en route to Gatwick Airport, are probably foreign, probably don't read English that well, and so probably don't know they shouldn't be in this section of the train. The child is also making a dreadful wailing sound, and a terrible mess of the table in front of him with spilt juice and crisps, which he has also now managed to get on the seat. Then there are the two pseudo businessmen in cheap looking suits who can't be bothered to wear a tie; surely they don't belong in here. There is a youngish man wearing sunglasses and headphones nodding his head to whatever rubbish he is listening to; no way is he first class material. Opposite him are two young women chatting to each other waving their arms around by way of expression; genuine first class people just wouldn't do that! Then there is the smartly dressed old man who looks the part, but I have seen him in the second class section before so he is just trying his luck; hence the worried expression on his face, and the fact he visibly jumps every time the corridor door makes a sound. There is also a big fat woman with huge legs dressed in a beige crimplene sack. She probably can't stand up for long, so assumes she can sit where she likes regardless of her ticket. Rarely seen in public these days, there is even a rosy-cheeked vicar wearing a soiled white blazer and looking very smug or possibly tipsy; surely his 'new church roof fund' could be better spent. Worst of all, there are three other people standing in addition to me, and I can see it is going to be a scramble to get a seat if any become vacant at the next stop. Oh where is the ticket inspector to fine, arrest, and eject all these dreadful imposters? Why oh why was I so stupid as to buy a first class ticket in the first place, and so subject myself to so much torment?

We are now past what was the next stop. As I suspected, the pseudo businessmen left the train only for their seats to be grabbed by two of the other people standing; and by the time the smartly dressed old man had decided he would get off as well, and then got in my way, a new smartly dressed old man had joined the train and taken the 'old' smartly dressed old man's place. Worse still, there are now vacant seats in the second class section so I can sit down if I want; but then I am wasting having paid the extra for my first class ticket, and all the 'nice honest people' who have taken **my** seat will have won. Even more worse still, because I **am** still standing, it has now become obvious that I am probably the only person to actually possess a first class ticket, and I can see all the 'nice honest people' smirking to themselves, and enjoying having thoroughly ruined my day. Oh why isn't this 1930's Germany, and I am a senior Wehrmacht officer, and I can strut back and forth in my highly polished boots whilst slapping my thigh and brandishing my Luger, and can order my men with their smart uniforms and Schmeisser machine pistols to clear the carriage of all this detritus, shouting 'Raus, Raus', as they do so. But I am deep into the realms of fantasy, once again.

Last Christmas, it was a different story. I was on holiday; I was in a very relaxed and philosophical frame of mind; and I was enjoying a head full of new scientific learning and deep ideas. Life is too short for all this stress. So what if the 'nice honest people' think they have won, does it really matter? I will go and sit in the second class section, having learnt my lesson, and reflect…

THE FAR SIDE OF THE WORLD

For the final leg of our South American adventure, my wife and I spent Christmas enjoying an amazing tour of the Galapagos Islands. The Galapagos consist of 13 major islands; 6 smaller islands; and scores of islets and rocks, lying either side of the Equator, 500 miles west of the mainland of Ecuador. Their total land area of 3,000 square miles is half the size of Wales but spread over an area of the Pacific Ocean half the size of England. The most sensible way to explore the Galapagos is therefore by boat, just like Charles Darwin did aboard the Beagle in the 1830's, a voyage that changed everything!

We had thankfully chosen a small vessel for our expedition which berthed twelve people in addition to the regular Ecuadorian crew and our local guide. Although this meant we would be living on top of our fellow passengers for a week, it had the huge advantage of their only being a small party of us every time we stepped ashore, and gave us the added opportunity to closely observe our own species whilst in a 'Darwinian' frame of mind.

Eight of our twelve specimens were of North American origin and of the same family, and here I will break with recognised taxonomy and refer to them as *Familia Waltonus,* because in many respects they reminded us of that television based mountain clan of 'Goodnight John-Boy' fame. The senior male *Waltonus* had with him his wife, and his son and daughter-in-law from a previous marriage. The wife also had with her, her son and daughter-in law from a previous marriage; and with the senior male had managed to produce a new offspring, now grown into a precocious and very spoilt 'all-American' teenaged brat. The final member of *Familia Waltonus* was a distinctly morose and suicidal bearded man in his thirties, who seemed to be some sort of floating relation of indeterminate status; possibly a parasite.

In addition to our two good selves this left two other specimens to be classified. Both of these were young ladies who seemed to be enjoying a symbiotic relationship. They also appeared to have misread Darwin's works and were working on their own alternative description of *Natural selection - survival of the fattest*! I shall label them as *Giganticus Australis* and *Giganticus Californicus* which also helps to pinpoint their normal habitat, although pinning either of them into a collection would have required an iron girder.

As with all good journeys ours started with a log. This was a 'fotographic' log (*sic*) for the sole benefit of *Mrs. Waltonus* who it turned out was celebrating a special birthday, and had treated the whole family to this holiday of a lifetime. First we had to watch all the family members smile at each other as they were duly snapped. Then they were snapped with the crew; then with each of us other guests; then with the family members again; and then the entire process was repeated because *Mrs. W* was not in enough of the shots, having been behind the camera most of the time. And then the entire process was repeated yet again, because *Mr. W* who had stepped in as official photographer had been doing it with 'attitude', and *Mrs. W* was very vocal with her displeasure further reinforced by her continued stamping. Although to us and most of the crew observing it was akin to being in the audience at a live situation comedy, we could, even at this early stage, tell that the rest of the family were wearing distinctly forced smiles and only on sufferance as she was paying for everything. Side comments such as 'Oh God, not another one Marmy', 'For f***'s sake woman!', and one of the elder daughters holding her own hair above her head as if to rip it from its roots helped to reinforce that impression.

Each day of our adventure followed a fairly strict itinerary. We would be woken early for a coffee (and fotos), the boat having travelled to a fresh destination during the night and then dropped anchor in the early hours. Activities would start with a snorkel, either off the boat, or if there were large sharks in the water, away from the main vessel and off one of the two rubber z-boats carried on board. Waiting to swim with us would be one or two female sea-lions sitting patiently on the rear of the vessel. Unlike sea-lions from the storybooks however, none of our playmates were ever balancing balls on their noses; instead, once in the water, they would swim around you, bite your flippers, bump into you, come at you at high speed from a distance, and generally add to the enjoyment or terror dependent upon your inclination. Personally I love sea-lions. I remember as a little boy often visiting Brighton Aquarium and making a point of always going to see and talk to the lonely sea-lion in her far too small Victorian era pool, no longer wanted or loved by the children since the arrival of the show-off dolphins. For some reason because sea-lions are large animals I always imagined she was a male, and this impression was no doubt reinforced by the fact she was called Fred. It would not be long before I would learn to tell the difference!

A much welcome hearty breakfast would follow our return to the boat after which we would commence our first island visit of the day. With luck and being on such a small craft, we would be the only people ashore. Occasionally however, one of the large cruise ships would anchor nearby and land its party of mostly

American tourists. Generally the first act of many of the older heavily perfumed females in these parties, was to pick up and cuddle one of the adorable and completely docile sea-lion pups that languish lovingly at your feet, staring at you with huge puppy-dog eyes.

'Photo me Honey!' they would chant to their fat clown-suited husbands, at the same time wondering why we and the local guides were giving them such foul and hateful looks. It is made very clear to you on entering the islands that you **'look and do not touch'**. Once picked up and given your scent, the pups are instantly rejected by their mothers and left to die of starvation; there are hundreds of them in this sorry state.

Back aboard for lunch the boat would move off to another island and we would enjoy sitting in the sea breeze; looking for passing turtles, whales and dolphins, and admiring the giant red-throated frigate birds that seem to follow all the vessels, floating majestically on an invisible current of air no more than a few feet above your head. One day we even enjoyed the temporary, but ethereal company of that most majestic of planetary travellers, an Albatross.

A further snorkel and another island visit would conclude the afternoon, the evening given over to a pleasant buffet dinner; watching the obligatory foto session descend into farce; enjoying the magical sunset; seeing the animal contingent board ship as darkness reigned; and an early night tucked up in a cosy dream-filled bunk bed; feeling rather than hearing that comforting throb of turbine; as the boat set off on dreams of its own, trailing phosphorescence beneath a breathtaking heaven of stars

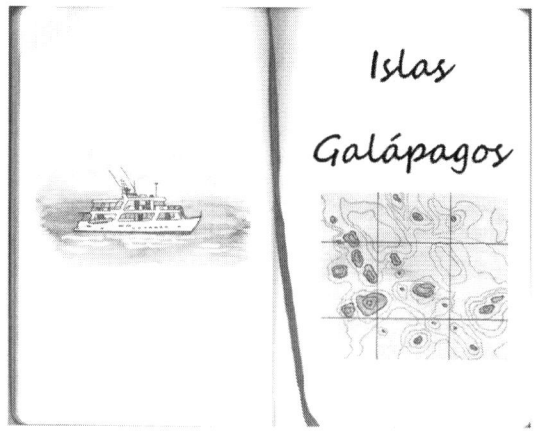

THE FOURTH ROCK FROM THE SUN

One dawn morning we visited the tiny island of Rabida which looks just like the Martian landscape photographed by the clever little NASA robot rovers, trawling slowly across its rocky surface some eighty million kilometres from planet Earth. Rabida's red iron rich soil matches that of Mars, and when viewed at sunrise the pink sky and barren nature of this little piece of land complete the comparison, but for the background presence of the Pacific Ocean. Mars of course has no oceans today, but there is proof positive that water once existed in abundance on its surface, creating the same water-driven geologic features we see here on our own planet, down to the scale of rounded pebbles.

In 2004, another very small robot was due to land on Mars with a very special mission – to search for life. The space-craft was British and called Beagle2 in honour of the Beagle that took Darwin to the Galapagos on his own voyage of discovery. Unfortunately all contact with Beagle2 was lost just after it parted from its mother-ship in orbit around Mars and, unless someone literally trips across it one day, we will never know what, if anything, it discovered and possibly tried to tell us about.

What Beagle2 was sent to look for was compelling evidence of microbiological life. The sort of microscopic blobby stuff that gets blobby microbiologists very excited, but which most of us find boring because we can only see it through a powerful lens or in a photograph, and in any event it just looks like, well, blobs. Most of the time, beneath each footstep you make, you are treading on a trillion or so of these micro-blobs. Instead, go into your garden or park and pick up just one tiny petal or blade of grass; something tangible you can see, feel, possibly smell, and even taste if it is herbal. Hold it in the palm of your hand, sit somewhere quiet and comfortable (choose a nice day!), and try and ignore all the other greenery, insects and life going on around you. Now try and imagine if you can that you are on Mars, sitting down on the dusty red soil but all cosy, safe and warm inside your multi-million dollar spacesuit. Outside your little safe haven, it is a cold, hostile world, teeming with deadly cosmic rays. You can see curiously shaped rocks and boulders, and massive but extinct volcanic peaks towering up into the pink-hued black starlit sky, far bigger than anything on Earth; but to all intents and purposes it seems you are completely surrounded by red nothingness, and quite, quite alone. Then you see a little green speck of life, just like you are holding now.

What you have in your palm looks so simple but is in fact massively complex. It is the result of billions of years of evolution. It contains its own incredibly long unique DNA signature, some of which is the exact same as some of yours; (in fact if you could stretch out all the

DNA in your new green friend it would reach to Mars and back again!); it has cells with walls through which gases are exchanged as the plant respires; it can take in sunlight and use this as part of its energy production process; it can even reproduce. In fact it is nothing short of a miracle and something we, with all our vast knowledge, incredible technology, and the best minds that have ever lived, have no idea how to create – life! Where **did** life spring from, and **how**?

The impact of finding something/anything that here on Earth is deemed so insignificant, living on or having lived on Mars or any other planet; or in fact anywhere else in the Universe would be phenomenal. It would certainly make global headlines for weeks to come, get nearly everybody on the planet talking and speculating, create some serious headaches for many in the religious fraternity, and give some people with strange hair and weird clothes the 'I told you so' chance of a lifetime. But in reality it really **would** change everything, and certainly the way we perceive ourselves. I certainly believe there must be life elsewhere in the Universe; countless life. Probability statistics positively dictate that there must be life elsewhere, the Universe is so uncomprehendingly vast, and most if not all space scientists would agree; but there is no denying the fact that to date, we have no evidence of life ever having existed on anywhere other than Planet Earth. **Would it change you, finally knowing for sure that we are not alone?**

Our Galapagos version of Mars hosted some giant-size and multi-hued amphibious lizards which marched about in prehistoric style, and looked similar to the ones film makers used to nail wings and glue horns to in early 'pre-politically correct' monster movies. As with all these sorts of things, we photographed the first lizard we saw - a small, dull coloured one in case it was the only one we were to see. Then we snapped a bigger red one; then we came across a large yellow monster; then a huge green dragon appeared, and then a large family group playing near the shore that we were able to swim and dive with. Back aboard our boat however, we could see all was not well in the *Waltonus* family group and a split was already forming. In fact, one of the younger couples decided to join our table for lunch as they had had enough of Marmy and her fotos for the day, and we didn't mind this a bit. Up until then the *Gigantici* had been sitting with us (or squeezing with us to be more precise, as the tables were small with fixed benches and all screwed to the floor making them immovable), and watching them scoff their food and talk at the same time didn't do anything for our own appetites! In fact watching them snuffle breakfast that morning had made me feel physically sick, only made worse by the antipodean *Giganticus* revealing she wasn't sure she should be eating at all as she had violent diarrhoea. What fun for the surrounding marine life!

Isla Rábida

area 4.9 sq km (lat 0.41, lon 90.7)
has distinctly Martian appearance
with iron rich soil
marine iguana
(ambtyrhynchus cristatus)
Tan, red, yellow, green

Flamingos
Pelicans
Blue footed Boobies

CRETACEOUS PARK

Early the next morning we found ourselves anchored offshore of a large island with an inlet leading inland. It was just after sunrise and a low mist hung over the island with the rainforest canopy appearing mysteriously above it. Approaching the island in our z-boats the azure Pacific turned to an emerald green lagoon as we crossed the inlet, and as our guide cut the engine, a family of giant stingrays appeared next to our boat and glided past with that slow majestic sweep of their wings that only rays can. The lagoon itself was surrounded by mangroves and black ooze with nowhere we could safely land; so we sat peacefully in our boat being warmed by the morning sun; marvelling at the multi-coloured birdlife; listening to the loud buzz of early morning insects; and looking for more marine life in this ancient untouched World.

My wife and I are avid *Doctor Who* fans, and looking around us I wondered what it would be like to travel to an island such as this but millions of years back in time, let's say 95 million years to the epoch we call the Cretaceous. For one thing, if I was approaching Earth in my *Tardis* from space, the planet would look very different from the one depicted by the globe in my study; I may not even recognise it as Earth at all!

There would be no ice caps to speak of; sea-levels up to an incredible 100 metres higher than today mean there would be far less landmass, with much of the land available today covered in shallow seas, and the continents themselves would be more grouped together than they are today, with markedly different coastlines. I would in fact be visiting Greenhouse Earth, a planet in a state far in advance of the 'greenhouse effect' we worry about today. It would however be a planet absolutely teeming with life, some of which may look familiar, but most of which would be as alien to us as anything Hollywood has ever dreamt up. From the fossil record we can determine just how strange and complex some of these creatures were, and just how giant; for this was of course an age of dinosaurs, the massive reptilian monsters that ruled both land and possibly the sea. Standing on my 95 million years ago planet, it would seem to me incredibly far back in time from where I started, but in fact it would be hardly any time at all in the grand scheme of things. From what we think we know, life first somehow appeared on Earth four billion years ago. After an incredibly long two billion years, life had evolved from simple bacteria (blobs), to slightly more complex cell-based life; and after another billion years had become multi-cellular algae that had discovered sex! Wind forward another 500 million years and life is still confined to the seas with multi-cellular jellies and sponges dominating, but still with no hard parts or shells. Then things start accelerating. Battles start raging between different species as they evolve ever more sophisticated weapons and armour; plants evolve and start to colonise the land; insects appear on the scene; animals finally step ashore and take to the land, even our own primitive mammalian ancestors join the evolutionary train; plants with flowers colour the landscape; and then we get to where I am 95 million years ago.

Despite the noise and hubbub all around me there is of course no-one and nothing I can communicate with, certainly nothing obvious that seems to have the intelligence I have; but then in our own time, do we really understand how whales and dolphins communicate and how intelligent and sophisticated they may really be? I feel like a visitor from outer space, everything is so strange and unlikely. Is this how an alien race, far superior in evolution to mankind would feel arriving on our own planet? Would they bother to communicate with us? Or would they just catalogue and observe us along with all the other creatures that inhabit the Earth?

I can hear something rustling in the undergrowth. If I am patient I will see that it is a tiny shrew. I can also hear much larger creatures approaching, smashing through the foliage and shaking the ground as they pound towards me – possibly raptors or something even more nightmarish. It is time for me to head back to the relative safety of my own time zone, but I hope my shrew escapes as well; after all, in another thirty million years time, a combination of massive volcanic out-gassing and a direct hit from a giant asteroid are going to create an extinction event across the entire planet. Although it might take tens, if not tens *of thousands of years, all the large dinosaurs will die out and it will be the turn of mammals, evolving from the likes of my shrew who will dominate, and from which we will finally emerge as modern humans some 200,000 years before the present day. (Incidentally, one reptile that did survive that catastrophe, and possibly due to its having a shell, was the tortoise, giant examples of which inhabit the Galapagos; the most famous being 'Lonesome George', whom we visited but who sadly passed away in 2012.)*

*That all important extinction event was 65 million years ago and it **did** change everything. I wonder what would have happened if it had never occurred? Would mammals have evolved as they did? Would mankind ever have evolved from primitive apes, having to compete with such fearsome adversaries? Would primitive apes even have had a chance to evolve in the first place? Or would the raptor dinosaurs have continued to evolve and begat an intelligent reptilian master-race capable of developing their own technology – the sort of little green men Martians were always depicted as in the 1950's?*

That afternoon we once again anchored offshore of the island, but further along the coast where we encountered a beautiful coral beach dotted with families of sea-lions. The boat needed to go off and re-provision, so the plan was that we spend an hour or two sunbathing on the pure white sands, and then snorkel back to the boat when it returned later in the day.

We were careful not to approach too near to the sea-lions as they had their young with them. In addition there were two massive male sea-lions, one at each end of the beach marshalling their harems. These monsters were at least three times the size of their female counterparts and hugely intimidating compared to Fred of Brighton Aquarium days. We could stand and watch from the shallows however, and at the same time enjoy experiencing small reef sharks swim between our legs!

Whether it was the heat of the day or just an overload of testosterone, suddenly the two beachmasters decided it was time for a battle. Seeing two giant blobs of fat approaching each other at speed and then clashing together in a noisy, violent and bloody embrace was awesome. Even more startling was watching them flump to the shore, faster than I would be able to run, and then power out to sea leaving behind a wake reminiscent of a torpedo; the speed was truly jaw-dropping.

Likewise observing this titanic coming together was our guide who had come to tell us it was time to snorkel out to the boat, which was anchored round the headland, not being able to get any nearer due to the low tide. When we were a few tens of metres from the shore, he swam over and gestured to my wife and I to tread water. The American *Giganticus* had latched onto us as her friend was apparently in a state of abject misery, and had stayed in her cabin (not to be seen again), and she was swimming just ahead of us. In her black one-piece costume and with her huge bulk, our guide was genuinely concerned that one of the male sea-lions would mistake her for one of his harem and attack us if we got too close. Worse still he may even see her as a rival bull and zero in to the attack like a guided missile. Having been duly told to hang back and keep a good distance, you know you are very scared and under immense stress when in addition to your heart racing, you can feel yourself sweating heavily despite being in cold water! Expecting something horrific to happen any second, we were both mightily relieved when minutes later the z-boats came roaring towards us to take us back to the ship. A huge three metre long bull-shark that had shadowed the vessel since the day before was now circling the craft waiting for nourishment, and it wasn't planned for any of us to be on its menu. (The bull-shark is closely related to its cousin the great white shark, only far more aggressive, and highly likely to attack!)

As we scrambled awkwardly but gratefully over the side of our z-boat we realised we had never tried landing the G*iganticus* who was now bobbing alongside, and becoming increasingly agitated as she sensed our collective concern. But despite the combined effort of the crew and ourselves, coupled with the G*iganticus* kicking frantically, there was no way we were going to be able to pull her aboard without the risk of capsizing. There was nothing for it but to drag her along half submerged, get the ship's cook to throw scraps to the bull-shark as we sped to the rear steps, and whilst the shark was otherwise engaged, push the *Giganticus* unceremoniously onto the ship. As she lolloped off in a state of utmost distress, it seemed more than likely that despite my initial glib remark upon first encountering them, there would now be two very large members of our species who would stay well and truly 'pinned' below deck.

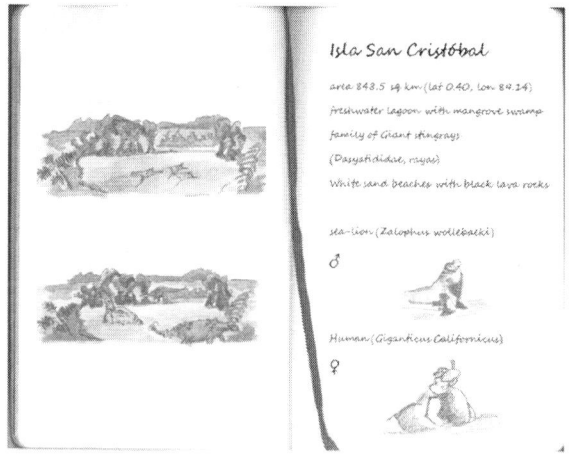

Isla San Cristóbal

area 843.5 sq km (Lat 0.40, Lon 84.14)
freshwater lagoon with mangrove swamp
family of Giant stingrays
(Dasyatididae, rayas)
White sand beaches with black lava rocks

Sea-lion (Zalophus wollebaeki)
♂

Human (Giganticus Californicus)
♀

THE DARK SIDE OF THE MOON

The following morning found us approaching the small island of Bartolome renowned for its lunar landscape. Although all of the Galapagos islands are volcanic, this small haven is more recent and therefore maintains much of its grey and grainy soil.

Obviously, you need a giant leap of the imagination to fool yourself that you are actually on the Moon's surface, but if you are sufficiently silly and take giant steps, lifting your knees really high and walk very, very slowly, it sort of creates the impression (including making nice impressions in the dust not unlike those the astronauts made, apart from the fact that I was barefoot due to the same type of boots they wore not being readily available, and the dust being completely different, and there being an atmosphere, and gravity being stronger here on Earth, and in fact they weren't anything like the same at all.) Talking in an out of breath metallic drawl and mentioning 'Houston' a few times also helps the deception; until you realise that not only your fellow man, but all the creatures on this lovely island have stopped whatever they were doing, are looking at you as if you are an imbecile, and are feeling very sorry for the lady standing well away from you and pretending not to be your wife.

By now we could observe that the *Waltonus* clan had split into two planetary systems; one orbiting around the father and his moody son; and the other orbiting mother which included an increasingly 'bored with life' brat; the prospective suicide having become a loner of sorts, and spun off into his own orbit which would take him into some deep dark recess of his mind. It seemed only at 'foto' time would they come together as a 'binary system', and even this was becoming less frequent and not without much dissention and outright hostility including the use of lewd hand gestures behind mother's back.

Whilst we and Mother's 'system' followed the well demarcated and well kept path around this small haven, coming to within inches of nesting birds which showed so little interest in us we might as well have been on the Moon, Father's 'system' seemed far more interested in the litter of driftwood, broken branches and bits of plastic, no doubt washed ashore by a recent tropical storm. Father W was even waving a stick around, as if conducting the smartly dressed penguin perched conveniently nearby, or perhaps he was re-enacting the golfing episode made famous by Apollo astronaut Alan Shepard.

Hundreds of birds, interesting animals, a refreshing swim, and a wholesome lunch later, I was sitting on deck staring at this lonely island, and quite naturally ruminating on things of a lunar nature which led to some 'out of the box' thinking indeed:-

You can't look at the smiling face of the Moon and not be reminded that mankind has actually been there and stood on its surface. If I had a choice of just one heavenly body to visit however, the Moon would not rate highest on my list. At ground level, it's a bit like most Southern English people imagine a Northern English seaside town to be in Winter-time. It's cold, grey, drab and gloomy; it's dead; there's a lot of junk lying around; it has a distinctly dark side; and someone has already been there, and written about it. The one huge difference being that instead of a grim overcast sky, the Moon boasts a spectacular view of our beautiful blue Earth. It is sad to think that despite Man's such high hopes and aspirations, it is now two generations since we last physically left the comfort zone of our own planet.

*When I walk across London Bridge on my way into the City, I am always reminded just how far mankind **has** advanced, but despite this, how little we have really changed. In that short 1000 feet in length crossing you can evidence over 1000 years of man's history: the Tower of London dating back to the Norman conquest of Britain, the host of so many Royal triumphs and tragedies; a replica of Francis Drake's Golden Hind in which he was the first English captain to circumnavigate the globe (and fill the Tower of London with captured Spanish Gold); the replica of Shakespeare's Globe Theatre in whose plays, veiled in allegory, Francis Drake got more than a few oblique mentions; the Monument to the great fire in 1666 which led to a rebirth of London; majestic St.Paul's cathedral,*

266

Christopher Wren's masterpiece – survivor of that great conflagration as well as of WW1 Zeppelin bombers, and Hitler's Blitz; Lloyd's of London, the site of the birthplace of insurance to support early 'globalisation', and home to many of Admiral Nelson's finest treasures; moored alongside Tower Bridge (the bridge which insurers oddly class as a ship and which most tourists confuse with London Bridge), HMS Belfast the WW2 battle-cruiser that without even needing to have physically viewed its target (so acting as if 'a hand of God') could have single-handedly wiped out the entire French and Spanish armada which cost Nelson his life, but which is now as obsolete as Nelson's flagship HMS Victory; modern day monuments to commercial success such as the Gherkin and the Shard; the flashing lights of countless aircraft queuing to land their globe-trotting passengers at London Heathrow or London City airports; and on the bridge itself – the site of Nancy's steps, immortalised by Charles Dickens in his dark, but comedic Victorian tale, Oliver Twist.

I wonder how Dickens would take to strolling with me across the motor traffic-laden bridge and seeing this 21st century City. Sitting with him in an 'American chain' coffee bar, and summarising what I think has been notable since his death in 1870, would he be hugely impressed; suitably enthralled; dumbfounded but at the same time proud of mankind in general (as I am) at the massive scientific advances we have made, especially in medicine and technology? Would he welcome the changes we have brought about? Would he even believe we have sent men to walk on the Moon, and robots to

strange world's even more remote and unforgiving?
Would he instead be appalled at the number of conflicts
still raging despite the scale of the two World wars since
his death; the global political and religious unrest; the
human misery that still pervades despite his attempts to
bring it to the World's attention; the colossal –
seemingly unstoppable growth in global population; the
threatened environmental disaster that hangs over us all,
undreamt of in his time; the countless lessons unlearnt
and opportunities missed? I suspect however, that take
him into the bookshop in Leadenhall Market; show him
how globally popular his works still are; let him absorb
the shock of perusing his own awe-inspiring biography
on the internet; and then promise him a airplane ride
that will take him to any destination of his choice,
anywhere on the planet in a single day, and he will be
more than content to ditch the philosophising, and be
'happy as a sand-boy'. I don't think telling a similar tale
to either William the Conqueror or King Henry VIII
would have a similar effect however; after all they would
no longer be masters of all they survey; their quaint
London home has been dwarfed by modern skyscrapers,
and their own achievements both good and evil, dwarfed
by subsequent history and the titans and tyrants that
have since reigned.

Over dinner on our boat, father *Waltonus* had decided to join us with the moody son (John-Boy), and perhaps based on his own musing of the day's events, was in a similarly philosophical mood.

'I make all my own furniture back home' he informed us, his glowing eyes betraying a proud beaming smile concealed behind his otherwise dead pan countenance.

'Let me show y'all my work. I keep fotos of all my favourite pieces with me to show my boy here 'cos one day they will all be his. This is my **legacy**! Hey, we could even do a home exchange with you Brits, and you can come over and experience it all in person!'

This kindly man then handed over to us a set of well worn and dog-eared photographs, clearly intended to thrill and delight.

Once again I was taken back to my thoughtful wanderings over the achievements of the human race. I was looking at pictures of the sort of confused mess our time-traveller might watch early Man produce, given some animal intestine, a heap of old fallen (perhaps washed ashore) branches, and an unintelligible Chinese version of the *Readers Digest* guide to cabinet making. This really was the sort of furniture that lends itself most readily to a lighted match, but which some other, kinder, more refined folk may refer to as having 'rustic charm'.

Trying to suppress my innate soliloquy and so not give away my immediate thoughts, and at the same time desperately delving to find a suitably polite comment from deep in my memory-banks, I was fortunately pre-empted by the moody son, who must have picked up a brainwave from me, and exploded at his dad with the shock comment:

'Dad, how many more times! I hate this sort of crap rubbish! I have told you over and over I am a minimalist, and will burn the whole bloody lot when you die! F*** it - you call this a legacy? You really think these nice English people want to swap homes with you and have to sit and eat on all this prehistoric shit?'

We could still hear raised voices from up above as we sank into our bunks on the deck below and chuckled ourselves to sleep. I remember wondering if Neil Armstrong has a den full of rustic furniture in his own home – one small step.

Isla Bartolomé

area 1.2 sq km (lat 0.28, lon 90.55)
Volcanic LUNAR landscape
Lots of driftwood and washed up
broken branches - must have been
A recent storm

Galapagos Penguin
(Spheniscus mendiculus)
Sea Turtles (Cheloniordea)
Galapagos Hawk (Buteo galapagoensis)

GENESIS

One of the last islands we visited was Floreana which was actually quite populated, something we had not really expected, believing the whole Galapagos paradise to be set aside solely for our lesser fellow creatures. Despite this, and following well trodden paths away from humanity, we were soon in an area of forest, leading down to a long black beach speckled with green olivine crystals washed by a turquoise ocean. A wonderfully pleasant stroll past innumerable sea-lions, penguins, iguanas, and nesting birds, all of which ignored us, led us past an emerald, flamingo bedecked lagoon to the white sands of Post Office Bay. The bay is so named because in days of old, mariners on their way to the New World would put messages in a barrel on the beach, to be collected and taken by fellow sailors on their way home to the Old World. The barrel remains to this day (or a version of it), and you can still post letters there without a stamp, some of which will magically find their way to their recipient, courtesy of other tourists who sift through, looking for letters addressed to their home town. Unfortunately people have added to the barrel over the years, nailing on pieces of driftwood or just plain rubbish to the extent that whilst still quaint, it is also unsightly. No surprise then that our master of all things rustic spent an inordinate amount of time photographing this curiosity, no doubt with a purpose to creating an exact replica in his 'yard' to thrill and delight his neighbours, or even add to the wondrous legacy portfolio.

Stepping over large boobies sitting confidently and happily on their ground nests, dodging the odd young albatross, and having to sidestep large advancing lizards, I realised I had become quite used to how naturally tame all the animals are in the Galapagos, and how prolific. This is just what it must have been like for those early adventurers, being the first humans to step ashore on remote Pacific islands, and coming across animals with no prior fear of man. It is no wonder so many species were either devastated, or even made extinct by these hungry and often uneducated sailors, oblivious that a couple of hundred years later huge strides would be made to save those species still remaining, and to protect their habitats. Nineteenth century and earlier journals also relate tales of huge fish stocks, and whales of all species in abundance, seemingly throwing themselves at the hooks and harpoons of the fishermen, 'so keen were they to feed our hungry mouths'.

Sitting on the warm sand on our last full day in this Pacific paradise made me wonder just how long it would remain as pristine and unspoilt. Although the Galapagos are sparsely populated by most other countries' standards, the indigenous population will inevitably grow naturally with all the competitive pressures that are consequent, unless some sort of control is put in place. I wonder how many people thought the same of other wonderful parts of the World, two hundred years ago, and that are now teeming with humanity.

There are still many parts of the World where you can get an inkling of what it must have been like before the global population exploded; of these the Galapagos has to be the most well known. It is a sobering thought that as recently as the early nineteenth century when Darwin was walking these shores, the global population was one billion, thought at the time to be excessive. Now, the population of India alone exceeds that sum.

It would be nice to think (as many Genesis followers indeed do), that once upon a time there had to be just two people - two people who somehow magically appeared; who we could identify as true Homo Sapiens; and from whom everyone on the planet, regardless of race, skin colour, height, build, hair colour, eye colour, or even shape of nose, have all evolved. What would life have been like for such a couple? Would it have been the paradise as depicted in Genesis before naughty Eve tempted her only too gullible beau? For certain, most of the species of animals that would have existed, would have been as tame and fearless of Man as those on Galapagos today, and incredibly bountiful. Some of the others however would have been a living nightmare. Think of all the carnivorous animals on the African plains that could ruin your day; then greatly increase the size of all these predators because there is no-one to

273

cull them; now add sabre toothed tigers, huge violent bears, giant aggressive antelopes with giant whirling horns, and then arm yourself with nothing but a pointy stick and a stone or two – hardly a paradise full of sweet frolicking lambs and simpering fawns with big dewy brown eyes, as depicted in early Biblical engravings.

Our first real ancestors also had to deal with the other hominid competition. As recently as 30,000 years ago there were still large, ugly, scary-looking Neanderthals living on the planet. It is now thought that these distant cousins of ours were actually more evolved than us, and more intelligent - they certainly had bigger brains and a more advanced culture. But they obviously lacked something, because somehow we wiped them out; or did they have compassion, and we didn't? Incredibly, there were other ancient hominids around at the time as well – Homo Erectus, the early Man who supposedly walked out of Africa 1.5 million years ago was still around as recently as 28,000 years ago. Perhaps some of these strange, wild, early Men still exist in remote parts of the World giving rise to the legends of the Yeti or Bigfoot. We don't know what the global population would have been back in those days, but to put things into a time perspective, only 18,000 years later, Egyptians were already busy farming, raising domesticated animals, and building simple temples in the Nile delta, and probably having a far more relaxed time than they are in the early twenty-first century, especially in the over-crowded cities.

It is probably inevitable that modern man migrates towards the City. On a recent trip to the magical, unique, but very 'Third World' island of Madagascar, we visited charming villages in the remote, rural countryside. These villages had quaint well-maintained houses; a central well; a witch doctor to keep off evil spirits and cure all ills; happy, smiling, seemingly well-fed people; and a way of life that to most Westerners of middle-age and above appears at first glance to be idyllic. Unfortunately, we learned that almost without exception, the young men and women of the villages turn their backs on this assumed paradise as soon as they are able, and head to the magnet of the capital city, Antananarivo. The raw power that pulls them in, is the promise of electricity, a mobile phone, television, and all the 'must-have' technological wonders they crave, and which don't exist back home. Once inside the huge slum that awaits them however, they are trapped. Not only is there no honest work for them and nowhere fit to live, but having left and experienced a vastly different world, they are no longer welcome back in the village of their birth - they no longer fit in. It made us realise that if a sudden global natural catastrophe did happen (perhaps an unstoppable virus, or another large asteroid impact, or the current Ice-age taking a sudden turn for the worse, or most likely of all – the overdue eruption of the supervolcano that waits patiently beneath Yellowstone National Park in Wyoming USA), and the human race was literally thrown back into the 'stone age', it would be very hard if not impossible for the vast majority of the World to come to terms with. For some however, like those villagers, life might go on as usual – would they even notice the change? But then would our species cease to evolve? Would we become stuck in a time-warp as those people seem to be, and literally just become interesting specimens for one day alien visitors to catalogue? Is it inevitable that we as a species have to completely swamp our planet, before we either seriously take that great leap into the outer Solar System, or swallow some very nasty medicine to prevent what appears to be a looming self-made catastrophe?

Back on the beach an impending catastrophe was heading its way towards the *Waltonus* hominids. It was now a case of no-one in the family talking to anyone else, but instead, mumbling to themselves. It was a bit like the Biblical parting of the tongues in the Genesis 'Tower of Babel' story. Even the family 'foto' sessions had ceased to exist, only mother still taking the odd snap. It struck me that perhaps if they each sat on a separate Galapagos island long enough they would develop their own unique characteristics, just like Darwin's famous finches that started the whole evolutionary thought process in that great man's brain.

The *Waltonus* clan were still wrapped up in their 'Babelian' misery the next day. We had said farewell to our little floating home and its' crew, and had made our way back by plane to Quito airport on the South American mainland, with only mother *Waltonus* still bothering to 'snap' away, completing her fotographic log. We were in the process of individually saying

276

goodbye to the family members when suddenly the meteor struck! Mother *Waltonus* had had her camera stolen. She had left it for safekeeping with Mr *W* while she went to the toilet, and now it had gone. The poor woman was naturally beside herself, every single precious picture she had taken throughout the entire trip was on that camera. 'It was her husband's fault; he had done it on purpose because he hated her.' 'It was the children's fault because they were smirking and sniggering and obviously didn't care (which they were – and probably didn't), and they hated her too'. She burst into floods of tears and was not to be consoled, and no little wonder, poor woman.

Looking back on this event, I like to imagine that some local Ecuadorian took that camera because they desperately needed money. They had some hungry if not starving children, one of whom had a terrible debilitating illness needing urgent treatment, and this was a last desperate act because there is no welfare state, and because the authorities don't and can't care. Whatever the real story however; to sell that camera, some heartless person had to knowingly press 'erase', and wipe out the wealth of never to be repeated photographic memories of a wife, mother and stepmother on her once only trip of a lifetime. They probably pressed that delete button or chucked the memory chip in the bin without a care in the World, or a thought for anyone but themselves; and being in the arrivals lounge back from the Galapagos, they would have known that camera would have been full of such irreplaceable treasure.

One hundred and thirty years ago, a certain scientist just after Darwin's death, would have dared to suggest that the camera thief was inherently bad, a stain on Mankind, and that he/she should be compulsorily sterilised to eliminate any future chance of their genomes tarnishing the human gene pool. He firmly believed we were duty bound to step in and help nature in this great game called Evolution. That famous scientist was one Francis Galton, Charles Darwin's cousin, and he founded the now infamous science of Eugenics.

Isla Floreana

area 173 sq km (lat 0.41, lon 91.50)
black beaches with olivine crystals

Emerald green lagoon
Post Office Bay – white sands

Albatross on nest
(Phoebastria irrorata)
Galapagos Tortoise
(Chelenoidis nigra)

A TURNED WORM

Thoroughly enthused by our trip, one of the first things I wanted to do upon our return to the UK was to visit Darwin's home. Luckily for me, Down House is situated in South London and is well worth a visit, it being a designated national treasure and open to the public. (There is a train from London Bridge to Orpington station which is nearby – and also conveniently near the ponds where we blew up the boat in Danger UXB!).

Twenty years after his own trip to the Galapagos, Darwin finally published his work *The Origin of Species by Means of Natural Selection*, a copy of which I bought at his house, and have on my desk at home. Much of this work he must have produced sitting at **his** desk, staring out into his worm filled garden; and wondering and pondering. Next to his study is a small room with an old-fashioned and scary looking bath type contraption. Darwin was apparently not a well man with much speculation still as to the nature and cause of his illness. It is in this small room that he would be 'sorted out' when feeling unwell, and I cringe from the details and the horrid looking gastro-orientated instruments in use at the time.

That his life must have been somewhat stressful goes without saying; he fathered ten children, not all of whom lived; his works were to shake the World and be met with often violent and malicious criticism; his views tore apart religious thinking and would have been somewhat at odds with the views of his devoutly Unitarian wife (another cousin); and even today, there are groups who advocate Mankind's very existence being based upon 'creationism' and 'Intelligent Design' involving a higher being over Darwin's theories; some even dismissing evolution as 'a fairy tale for grown-ups'. Darwin must also have debated long and hard with cousin Francis, with his hard line views on how to shape the future of the human species, although this somewhat sinister side to Down House merits only the briefest of mentions on the house tour.

Francis' solution, Eugenics, is all about nurturing the human gene pool. That doesn't (or wasn't supposed to) mean 'ethnically cleansing' anyone, Balkan or Rwandan style; but it does mean identifying all types of people who, through hereditary traits, either add no value or are a burden to society; and sterilising them, or at least forbidding them from breeding with other 'purer' people. The aim of course, is that just as the farmer improves his herds, so a responsible society should weed out the weak and needy; the criminally minded; the insane; paupers; alcoholics; the general human detritus; and of course, people who travel in first class with a second class ticket. The upside for these unfortunates, is that most Eugenics programmes recommend that these individuals should be well looked after at state expense during their lifetime (sit anywhere you like, madam); on the basis that, 'once they're gone, they're gone', as the super-market strap-line goes.

This doctrine, anathema to modern thinking is so closely linked to that of Nazi Germany, it is oft overlooked that one of the many 'civilised' nations to embrace its ideals from an early age was the United States. In fact, at the Nuremburg war crimes trials, the Nazis cited the U.S. as their inspiration for adopting eugenics, and it wasn't until the 1960's that America stopped all state sponsored sterilisation.

The process of 'racial purification', goes back to Man's earliest recorded history; both Plato and Aristotle had much to say on the subject, and most major religions have had a good go at ridding the World of their competition at some time or another. Maybe this is what early Homo Sapiens was practicing with the Neanderthals, it just needed Francis Galton to come along and give it a nice scientific name, so it could then later on be outlawed.

Modern 21st Century medicine now offers mankind the real but somewhat scary opportunity to genetically engineer a better breed of human, even incorporating 'bionic' elements to enhance our powers and our senses, and maybe even one day being able to dictate our nature thereby creating an army of model citizens. There is a colossal moral issue to overcome in following this approach however, and many commentators see it as cheating evolution and Mother Nature. But then if we have evolved the knowledge to be able to engineer 'better' versions of ourselves, is this not evolution working at its optimum?

Charles Darwin is the man who firmly took the lid off this can of worms, and then strangely spent most of his life studying them; *Worms* being the final book Darwin had published before his death in 1892. It is therefore a shame he is buried in a stone sarcophagus within Westminster Abbey, for whilst being a fitting resting place for such a great Man, it does somewhat deny the relatives of his favourite of God's creatures, a tasty feast.

Down House

The study where
Charles Darwin wrote:
The Origin of Species
By means of
Natural Selection

I am sitting on the morning train to London Bridge. It is not quite the 7.52 as this train leaves ten minutes earlier than that; but I am looking out of the window and watching the countryside speed by relative to my position in space and time. If that sounds somewhat scientific, it may be because I **am** a scientist. Five long years have passed since I watched my daughter 'walk the walk' across the university stage, and I have now achieved the same; my hand being shaken by the Dean of my university, the film producer David Puttnam. It may also be because there is nothing I *have* to read, and so my mind is once again free to wander without any underlying sense of guilt.

This may well be one of the last times I travel as a regular commuter. Having a degree, especially a science degree, not only opens up a host of opportunities, it changes you. For one thing I have learnt how to learn, and in consequence of overcoming that most difficult of hurdles, I have discovered a vast amount about our planet Earth, how it was probably made, and where it fits into the grand scheme of our Solar System, our Milky Way galaxy, and beyond. I have learnt a vast amount about life on Earth, how life has managed to continue and thrive despite numerous global extinction events throughout Earth's long history; and how life has almost it would seem, miraculously evolved – Darwin's great revelation. I have learnt a vast amount about molecules and how they do chemistry together; about atoms and how they react together; and how everything including ourselves, is made from sub-atomic particles existing a fantastically strange life within a quantum world, that only the greatest brains can begin to comprehend. I have even learnt that somewhere in another universe the bizarre painting on the rear cover of this book is a photograph. But most of all, I have learnt a vast amount about me.

Incredibly, the Open University have asked whether I would consider a career as a science teacher in a secondary school, and I have agreed to give it a go. Swapping sleepy headed fellow commuters for sleepy headed youngsters will be interesting to say the least. No doubt I may well come across smaller but fast ripening versions of Tweedledum and Tweedledee, and almost assuredly have to contend with embryonic zygotes, unlikely gentlemen, and their counterparts. I have no idea what my fellow teaching staff will be like. Will they remind me of the tyrants I rebelled against when I was a pupil? Will they be predominantly female, and swarm like my bee ladies, or behave like a more educated coven of witches, or show their displeasure like the buxom hats? Will I actually get to know my fellow passengers on this new journey and make countless new friends? Or will I once again feel like the last man standing in a first class compartment, because I am different, and feel like I've arrived from a distant planet? Worst of all, I worry that despite having had forty years to mature, I might find myself to still be the naughtiest boy in the school.

I am going to focus on Physics, a subject I have come to love, but which is at odds with a belief in a spirit world I have been fortunate enough to see and touch. Marrying the two together may well provide a platform from which to commence a new challenge. One thing is for sure; the next five years are going to be every bit as stimulating as the last five, and if I change just half as much, I will hardly recognise myself.

But I am going to miss my fellow commuters; I even wish the Unlikely Gentleman was here to give me one last threatening look, and worry my suit with his filthy feet. Is he lucky? He will continue to read his stars and be content with the fortune Madame Astra predicts for him. I have to predict my own. There will be little time for staring aimlessly out of the window where I am going...

God Bless

TRIBUTES

I have borrowed or derived a number of 'Train No.' titles from other works to which I wish to pay tribute.

The alternative Railway Children - *The Railway Children by Edith Nesbit, 1905.*

Danger UXB – *ITV series developed by John Hawkesworth, 1979*

The World's Smallest Public Railway – *based on the original strap-line of the Romney, Hythe and Dymchurch Railway, http://www.rhdr.org.uk/index.html*

The Incredible Journey – *Sheila Burnford, 1961*

The Far Side of the World – *Patrick O'Brian, 1984*

The Dark Side of the Moon – *Pink Floyd, 1973*

The Fourth Rock from the Sun – *from 3rd Rock from the Sun, American sitcom, NBC, 1996 - 2001*

Cretaceous Park – *from Jurassic Park, Michael Crichton, 1990*

ACKNOWLEDGEMENTS

William Harrison Ainsworth - *quoted in Train No.6*

Charles Dickens – *quoted in Train No.6, Train No.7, Train No.15*

Gilbert and Sullivan (from HMS Pinafore) – *quoted in Train No.11*

'Lions and Tigers and Bears Oh No!' – *from Wizard of Oz, lyrics by Yip Harburg - quoted in Train No. 12*

Volcanoes, earthquakes and tsunamis – *David, A, Rothery, 2001 Teach yourself – quoted in Train No.12*

'Into the realms of fantasy' – *from Dads'Army by Jimmy Perry and David Croft - quoted in Train No. 10 and Train No.14 and to Dad's Army for spurring memories in Train No.9*

'Tardis' and 'Doctor Who', *from Doctor Who, British Broadcasting Corporation, mentioned in Train No.14*

'The Waltons', *from Lorimar Productions, 1972, quoted in Train No.14*

'Evolution is a fairy tale for grown-ups' – *from English Heritage, Down House Brochure, 2009, quoting Louis Bounoure, professor of biology at Strasbourg University writing in The Advocate, 8 March 1984. – quoted in Train No.14*

A special acknowledgement to:-

The Editor, my eldest daughter Alexandra Page for her professional, enthusiastic and hard work in (duly, of course and therefore) editing this book, and daring to justifiably delete some of the more lunatic elements which included a romance with a fish.

Crystal Palace Park for continuing to maintain and treasure the wonderful dinosaur statues that pre-date Darwin's publication, and that have inspired me ever since my push-chair days, http://www.crystalpalacepark.org.uk

The Open University – for teaching me the science. *The Open University, http://www3.open.ac.uk*

My late brother Paul James Kirkman-Page (the man behind the curtain) – for leaving me his endearing *'God Bless'*.

And to all of my family, wherever and whenever they may be – *for everything.*

ABOUT THE AUTHOR

Julian Kirkman-Page has spent most of his working life commuting to and from London Bridge station. He lives in the South of England with his wife, and when not in the City or writing, spends much of his spare time either being in, on or under water, exploring the planet, or walking along the sea-shore and wondering. He describes himself as a closet quantum physicist. He has two grown up daughters, three nieces, a grandson, and a sabre-toothed tiger called Scabby Fish-head.

If you have any questions or comments, or you would like to share information with me in relation to this book, please feel free to contact me via my website:-

www.the752tolondonbridge.com

19347731R00172

Printed in Great Britain
by Amazon